It Still TAKES a VILLAGE

Help for Parents in Dealing with Academic Underperformance

VIVIENE KERR, Ed.D

Kingston, Jamaica W.I.

. . . . .

Published by:
Extra MILE Innovators
21 Phoenix Avenue,
Kingston 10, Jamaica W.I.
www.extramileja.com

Editing: Kethjoy Watson
withornpublishing@gmail.com

Cover Design: Olivia's Pro-designer services

National Library of Jamaica Cataloging-in-Publication Data
Name: Kerr, Viviene, author

Title: It Still Takes a Village: Help for parents in dealing with academic under performance / Viviene Kerr.

Description: Kingston:
Extra MILE Innovators, 2021. | Includes bibliographical references.

Identifiers: ISBN 9789769674653 (pbk).

Subjects: LCSH:
Education – Parent participation. | Academic achievement. | Motivation in education. |Student adjustment.

Classification: DDC 370.1523 -- dc23.

Author Contact: For consultation, bulk orders, feedback or speaking engagements, contact the author at dr.vivienekerr@gmail.com.

I dedicate this book to the parents of children who are underperforming, the ones yet to be identified and for whom this assignment had to be completed. May the guidance provided here relieve the stress, shame and discouragement that threaten the parents and guardians of children who struggle with academic underperformance.

Acknowledgements

Why do students underperform? The answer to that and other related questions lie within the pages of this book, in which the Lord, my family and clients have awakened my interest. I pay tribute to them, as they taught me that it is possible to triumph over the pain of academic underperformance.

I thank the students and families mentioned herein and the members of the parent teacher's associations who afforded me the privilege of serving them and to explore possible solutions to the problem at hand. Thank you to Special Educators Tanee Lawson and Avril Gordon-Clarke and Licensed Counsellor Lorraine Smith who contributed to the chapter on Learning Disabilities.

Special thanks to my book and publishing coach Cameka Ruth Taylor, the editors, proofreaders and all who were directly involved in the preparation and completion of the text. Commendations to my family and friends who encouraged me to complete the publication amidst competing responsibilities which threatened the timely completion of the various sections.

Finally, to my colleagues, friends and supporters who recommended titles, and cheered me on towards the finish line. This project took longer than anticipated but the delay afforded me the opportunity to ensure its currency and relevance.

Introduction

Welcome to a greater understanding of academic underperformance. You will be taken on a journey as together we seek to explore the inner world of academic underperformance and how to help your child overcome it.

Academic underperformance occurs "when a student is working below their potential, i.e., they are working below their ability, or not achieving what they should be" (Ludovici, 2015, p.7). Children who underperform academically will exhibit certain behaviours and or attitudes towards their education.

As a Counselling Psychologist, Educator, and parent, I have witnessed the frustrations, disappointments and discouragement of both parents and students who have failed to achieve the expected outcomes from their academic pursuits. I have also seen how intervention and collaboration have enabled parents and teachers to help children excel. You will read of several cases and success stories in the subsequent chapters.

Like many parents, I am an extremely busy professional. Nevertheless, I decided to make the time to get involved in my children's education. This decision to get involved was because of my knowledge that parental involvement and expectations can significantly improve children's performance. I became an active member of my children's parent teachers' associations to lend my skills as a Counselling Psychologist to other parents. I was elected to leadership positions and furthered the agenda of parental participation and commitment in supporting their children's educational objectives and the schools they attend.

My mission is to deliver the message through these pages, that there are many reasons why students underperform. The key is to identify them, get help, accept it and build or repair your children's self-esteem, regardless of the difficulties. I encourage parents to celebrate the positives, fix the fixable, accept the unchangeable and enjoy the gift of parenthood.

Parents, you can help your children. There is hope and a way to do it. Your children can perform well no matter how daunting it seems.

We as a family have excelled academically despite the challenges of single parenting and the COVID-19 pandemic. My desire is to help others do the same.

Overview of the Book

CHAPTER 1 will provide a brief introduction to academic underperformance. We will begin with an explanation of the concept, a look at the statistics and examples within the locale where the book was written and the typical challenges that both children and their parents face as they are confronted with the issue of academic underperformance. The issue of learning disabilities and challenges that children face and the concept of multiple intelligences are mentioned along with a proven system for solving academic underperformance.

CHAPTER 2 will focus on collecting information in order to get a better understanding of how your child learns. Knowing and understanding the way your child learns will help you see the relationship between his/her dominant learning style and the best methods to use in teaching him/her or in helping him/her to study. This information is critical in identifying the reason behind your child's academic underperformance. You will be taught how to identify your child's dominant learning style and how to create a learning style profile as you seek to support learning at home.

CHAPTER 3 will guide you on how to get your child properly assessed. It will also explore the use of School Reports in identifying trends and patterns that may not have been identified or acknowledged and reinforce the need to get the foundation right in order to prevent problems at other levels of the education system.

CHAPTER 4 will offer specific tips for supporting learning at home. It will present strategies for the specific developmental and educational level of the child. The principles of family support are emphasized along with the need for parental participation within the child's school.

CHAPTER 5 will offer specific tips on preparing your child for external/final exams. It offers a few programme-specific outcomes/assessments and institutional expectations of children within the locale in which the book was written. The chapter will also explore various requirements and expectations of the institutions' examiners; such as PEP, CSEC, bachelor's, master's or doctoral degrees, theses or dissertations and institutional resources and websites.

CHAPTER 6 will examine your role as a parent in helping your child reverse academic underachievement. It will examine how to eliminate Learning Gaps such as those arising from the COVID-19 Pandemic.

CHAPTER 7 will cover learning disabilities and academic underperformance and will look at how to identify the common types of learning disabilities/challenges; what to do and how to help your child deal with learning disabilities.

CHAPTER 8 will share the success formula and how to identify your children's learning style as well as the development of their learning style profile (LSP). It will (i) explain how psychoeducational assessments (PEA) are done, (ii)present insight on how the identification/diagnosis (Diagnosis) of your child's problem is done, (iii) reinforce the importance of the grade report analysis (GRA) and of correcting identified problems to prevent additional ones and (iv) describe the development of a prescription for your child's success. It will conclude with an explanation of the formula [LSP+PEA+GRA = Diagnosis (D) + Prescription(P) + Remediation (R)].

CHAPTER 9 will tackle where to get help after exhausting school resources. It will introduce you to the tools for resolving the various problems identified. The concept of "the village" or team-based approach will be reinforced. The role of various professionals in resolving specific problems identified and the principle of collaborating with these professionals will be outlined. You will learn how to support your children's educational pursuits beyond the school environment. Other challenges such as medical, psychological, and socioeconomic problems that affect earning, retention and general academic performance will be explored.

CHAPTER 10 covers success stories and gives a brief synopsis of the academic journeys of the children/families mentioned within this book. Finally, the principle of acceptance will be outlined as there will be challenges that parents may not overcome.

A number of appendices have been provided. They include a learning style survey, checklist of academic underperformance, a directory of institutions/services available to assist you with your child who has learning disabilities and Learning and Retention Techniques/study skills.

Contents

Chapter 1

Introduction to Academic Underperformance

A Day in the Life of a Child Who is Underperforming

Analisa arrived at school and was informed that she would be getting a test. She was surprised, but relaxed, as she believed she was able to pass. They were given the textbook to revise the topics taught during the month leading up to the test. Just before they began, the teacher asked a student to collect the books from everyone. Analisa returned her book and the test began. At the end of the process, everyone, including Analisa, handed the papers to the teacher.

Later that day, Analisa's grandmother got a call from the teacher, who advised her that after all the children left school that day, she discovered one of the textbooks under Analisa's desk. She advised Analisa's grandmother that Analisa would be losing marks for cheating on the test.

Analisa's grandmother asked her about the test and what took place at school that day. Despite her protest about not knowing how the book got under the desk, she was penalized for cheating on the test, and given a stern warning about lying, cheating, and wanting to be first. Analisa explained that she believed it was a prank as her classmates are always teasing her about wanting to be first all the time. True to her word, the teacher gave Analisa a B+ instead of the A that she had earned.

This situation may not resemble a typical manifestation of academic underperformance. The general tendency when we speak about academic underperformance is to look at persons who are getting C's or Ds or failing. There are children who are doing very well academically, they may be getting good grades (Bs and B+s), when they could have been getting A's. Those students are beneath their capacity.

Academic underperformance does not necessarily speak to receiving failing grades, in the way we generally think about it. It speaks to children who can or could be doing better, if the situations that they faced daily, even within a school setting, helped or were different.

Analisa's grandma contacted me for assistance as she prepared her for the Primary Exit Profile Exam (PEP). Her request for assistance came as Analisa's teacher expressed concerns about a decline in Analisa's grades.

I agreed to provide both her and her granddaughter coaching services, geared at improving Analisa's performance. My work with Analisa involved reflections on her days at school. This is just one of the strategies I employed as I conducted a psycho-social assessment, aimed at identifying the cause of her academic deficit.

Where Are We Now?

Journey with me as we examine this matter from another sector of the education system where students seek to matriculate into university. The challenges facing them became very clear as I worked with one of our local universities. Every year, there was a challenge getting qualified persons to access the programmes. Generally, the number of CSEC subjects required for admission at that institution was five including Mathematics and English.

Year	5 including Maths and English A	5 including English A Only	5 including Maths Only	5 including Maths and or English A	% of Grade 11 Enrolment
2019	9234	4235	392	13861	38.2
2018	9566	3578	700	13844	36.2
2017	8703	3714	695	13112	33.5
2016	8699	3774	524	12997	33.3
2015	9979	2614	1080	13673	34.1

NUMBER OF SECONDARY LEVEL STUDENTS PASSING 5 OR MORE SUBJECTS INCLUDING MATHEMATICS AND OR ENGLISH A, 2015-2019 *

*Students would have sat and passed subjects in earlier grades

Data provided by the Ministry of Education Youth and Information (MOEYI) revealed that 38.2% of the 2019 cohort of Jamaican students passed five or more CSEC subjects including Mathematics and or English A (P. Gordon, personal communication, November 11, 2021), the minimum requirements needed to seamlessly matriculate to the tertiary sector. As a country, we have long recognized that there is a problem. Low matriculation into universities was traced not just to the high school, but to the primary level and sometimes beyond to the early childhood level (MOEY, 2017). Analisa's story provides an illustration of what is likely to happen without intervention.

To correct the problem, the Ministry of Education, Youth and Information (MOEYI) has had to implement measures as far back as the early childhood level. Research has shown that if a child has underperformed from the beginning of the school system, the trend will continue all the way up to secondary level; hence the problem of inadequate students matriculating to the tertiary level. Some students even continue to underachieve during their university careers. That has serious implications for national development.

The Inner World of Parents with Children Who Underperform Academically

Let's return to Analisa's story. How would you feel as a grandmother who has been charged with the responsibility of preparing your grandchild for this external examination? Let's examine the world of the parents or the grandparent in this case.

Whenever I am approached to partner with parents who recognize that their children are underperforming, I make it very clear that I do not work with the children alone. I work with the parents and the children. If you are helping the children and they do not have the support of their parents or if the parents are unaware of how they can help, it becomes challenging and counterproductive.

Analisa's grandmother takes care of her family while Analisa's mother lives and works in rural Jamaica. She sends money to take care of Analisa's needs. Grandma is therefore accountable to her daughter in ensuring that Analisa does well at school. Grandma gets really frustrated when she gets a call from school about a child whose grades show that she is capable of doing better. Analisa's grandmother complained that the children at her school "pick on" her. In other words, her peers were bullying her. Analisa's grandmother always defended her as she was very quiet, nice, and soft-spoken. Her mild-mannered personality made it easy for the other children to bully her.

Another factor, in this case, is that Analisa was born and lived briefly in the USA and has an American accent. The children at school teased her about her accent, you know how it is in a primary school. Maybe if it were a preparatory school, it wouldn't be as bad, because they tend to speak in standard English.

As I examined Analisa's school environment we discovered that the bullying made her unhappy and affected her academic performance. She explained that she was always conscious that her classmates may tease or prank her. She became very fearful and discouraged and those emotional experiences created a longing to return to the country of her birth.

Let's return to grandma.

Analisa's grandmother was frustrated by the many complaints. She visited the school and asked that they do something because the bullying was affecting her granddaughter's schooling and learning. She explained that she was very forceful when she spoke with the teachers or school administrators. "I am not going to stop until you fix this thing!"

That peek into the world of Analisa's grandmother is quite a relatable story for several parents in Jamaica. As parents, we have had situations where you talk with the teacher, and it doesn't help. You visit the Vice Principal and you have to go all the way to the principal before justice is served. The world of parents is difficult if they want to be involved in their children's education to ensure that they perform optimally. They must be very persistent and prepared to do what they have to in order to ensure that Their children's needs are addressed.

Factors Affecting Academic Underperformance

Learning disabilities and other challenges associated with learning and retention will contribute to academic underperformance. Some children underperform because they have learning disabilities or other challenges and they need to get help in order to do well academically. The inability to focus or stay on task, being unable to learn and retain information needed to do well in assessments are factors that will affect academic success. These are neurological abnormalities that result in cognitive challenges that will also be explored later in Chapter 7.

Social problems faced by children within and outside of families may result in academic underperformance. These are manifested in psychological challenges of fear and anxiety from being bullied and or from poor parental practices. Yes, there are times when parents are not doing a good job and it affects their children adversely.

The important point to bear in mind is that there are several risk factors working together or individually that contribute to academic underperformance; not just the mental abilities of a child.

As you peruse these chapters, I will share the keys to academic success that will include several recommendations and solutions. I will also share my system of improving academic performance and how I have worked with various children moving them from a state of failure to success. I explore what happens within the classroom which I have referred to as "looking inside the black box". We will discover the role of teachers. Yes! Educators are contributors to academic underperformance!

In Analisa's story, her teacher believed that she cheated; and gave her a lower grade. The teacher's action resulted in a less than stellar performance on Analisa's school report. Teachers have a critical role to play in recording a student's true potential as assessed. If they do not execute that responsibility well, it can create an impression of academic underperformance.

Our children are gifted differently. There is a concept in psychology called multiple intelligences. It focuses on the uniqueness of individuals and that each child will perform differently in various areas of study. We need to bear that in mind as we assess children's true potential. You will discover that it is not always about academics. This means that as we look at underperformance, the focus is on the total child and how we can encourage their inherent gifts and talents. We will explore that concept further in an upcoming chapter.

Solving Academic Underperformance

When a child is underperforming academically, I recommend that you get a psycho-educational evaluation done. This assessment will reveal the source of the problem. Engage the services of a psychologist. There are Child Psychologists, Educational Psychologists, Counselling Psychologists and Clinical Psychologists who will interview both you and the child in order to identify the source of the dilemma. That professional will also work with you to develop a unique system to resolve your child's problem.

Obtain an assessment of your child's learning profile. This is a test that will be administered to reveal your child's dominant learning style. There are several tools available online to assess learning styles. When you have ascertained the dominant style of learning, share this with the teachers. They will utilize the information when choosing the most appropriate strategy to help your child learn. Details of this process will be provided in a chapter later on.

An analysis of past school reports must be conducted. This will reveal trends or patterns of weaknesses that you may have missed like "needs to pay attention in class". In identifying and strategizing to solve those areas of weakness, correcting those deficiencies will provide a stronger foundation on which to build. If significant areas of weaknesses are found, hire a tutor to provide the individual attention that is needed to hone that particular skill. Once mastery is attained, your son or daughter may advance to higher cognitive functions and tasks such as understanding a passage after learning to read well. If additional challenges are identified while the tutor works with your child or if the child is not advancing as expected, it may mean that the child has a learning disability that needs to be identified through psychometric testing at an approved assessment centre.

To solve your child's problem of academic underperformance, I would review the results of the assessments and tests conducted and prescribe or recommend a unique course of action. The details of that process and the recommended course of action will be discussed in subsequent chapters.

Chapter 2
Understanding Learning Styles

In this chapter, we will explore learning styles, teaching and study techniques. The following is a synopsis of the areas to be covered:

- Learning Styles and Parental Involvement
- Learning Styles and Learning Style Profiles
- Learning Styles and Teaching and Study Techniques

John and Michael are fraternal twins with different learning and academic profiles. John was a Spelling Bee champion and Michael was an average learner. Their parents were aware of their differences and were prepared to send them to the schools at which they had been placed, based on their Primary Exit Profile (PEP) external examination results. Both boys though placed at different schools, were very accepting of their placements based on their PEP results. The family believed that the schools would best cater to the boys' individual differences.

Despite this knowledge, their mother was encouraged to seek a transfer for the one who had been placed at a recently upgraded non-traditional high school. Others encouraged her to apply for a transfer to the traditional high school that his twin brother would attend. She became confused and called to discuss with me the wisdom of doing what others were recommending. We discussed the results of the psychoeducational assessment that I had done for both children prior to their external examinations and her commitment to trust the wisdom of the education system and the placement that would result from their exam results. She thanked me for the reminder and refused to apply for the transfer.

Learning Style Profiles: Identifying Your Child's Dominant Learning Style

We are all different. We have unique ways of learning and retaining information. Have you noticed these differences in each of your children or between yourself and your child? Do you know the easiest way to teach your child to know, remember or do something? That is your child's dominant learning style.

Learning styles refer to the understanding that every student learns differently. Technically, an individual's learning style refers to the preferential and fastest way the student absorbs, processes, understands, retains, and uses information.

There are three dominant learning styles: auditory, visual, and kinesthetic.

Auditory learners prefer to listen to instructions and are able to retain the information by reading it aloud. Some may study while listening to music, while others may be easily distracted by noise and need a quiet place to study. Among the strategies recommended for helping auditory learners are (a) talking with them about what they are learning, (b) recording and playing back information taught, (c) listening to audiobooks, (d) word associations, (e) making songs about lessons taught and (f) reducing distractions during study times.

Visual learners like to read, look at graphics and watch demonstrations. They prefer illustrations and become impatient during long oral presentations. They are best assisted with flash cards, charts, tables, maps, illustrations and reviewing notes taken in class. Highlighting, underlining and other visual cues like colour coding works best for them.

Kinesthetic learners like to do things while studying. They will read and make notes to keep awake, highlight, and use colour codes, walk while reading, tap their feet while sitting to read a book, take frequent breaks and create models of concepts being taught. It is not always easy to support kinesthetic learners as they need activities such as games and other creative activities in order to remain engaged and to remember concepts taught.

While your child may have a preference in the way he/she learns, please keep in mind that he/she may use a combination of styles. They may also learn different things in different ways and their dominant learning style may change as they get older.

There are several tests online that can help you to determine your child's dominant learning style. *Please see Appendix A for one such test which is usually administered to young children.* A learning style profile is a composition of the child's dominant learning style, his/her strengths, and weaknesses, that which motivates him/her to learn, his/her academic aspirations and other personal data related to their learning experience and needs. A learning style profile includes attention to intelligence preferences and cultural and gender differences. As parents, we need to know our children's learning styles and be able to create a profile of how they learn.

When you know how your child learns and what helps him or her to absorb, process, understand, retain, and use information, you will be able to help him or her grasp concepts faster and thus reduce your and his/her frustration. Understanding how your child learns can reduce frustration and improve his/her academic achievement.

Learning Styles, Teaching and Study Techniques

There is a direct positive relationship between a child's dominant learning style and the strategies that are used to teach him or her something new. Some children learn faster if you create a song to help them remember the lesson. Others like to read books that explain the concept. Some students learn by playing a game or making an object to fully understand an idea or concept that is being explained. In addition to learning, children must remember what they have been taught.

Teaching them using tools and or techniques that cater to the way they learn best will help them to remember what is being taught. Encourage your child to spend time and attention on studying to achieve peak performance. A child who does not learn or study that which is taught will underperform. There are several techniques that can be used to enhance study. The ones that you or your child choose, should match your child's dominant learning style. If there is a disconnect between the learning/study techniques and the learning style, they may underperform academically.

Chapter 3
Proper Assessments

In this chapter, we will explore psycho-educational assessments, school reports and how to identify areas of underachievement in your child. The following is a synopsis of the areas to be covered:

• Psycho-educational assessment and the psychology of learning

• Grade reports and their role in revealing challenges

• Understanding your child's true potential in order to gauge your expectations

• Parent/Teacher collaboration

• Checklist -Is your child underperforming?
  – Why you need to know
  – What you need to do about it

• Supporting learning at home

Psycho-Educational Assessment and the Psychology of Learning

P sycho-educational assessments are geared towards the examination of the psychological and educational conditions that may affect learning, retention, and the application of information/knowledge. Let us explore the concept of the psychology of learning as we seek to understand the relationship between conducting a psycho-educational assessment or evaluation and the solution to learning challenges. The psychology of learning focuses on how people learn and interact with their environments. Psychologist John B. Watson stated that all behaviours are a result of the learning process. Albert Bandura developed the Social Learning Theory which states that learning takes place within a context and the learning environment affects a child's ability to learn, retain that which is taught and ability to use the knowledge that has been gained.

Educational Psychology focuses on:

1. The learner

2. The learning process

3. The learning situation or environment

4. The teacher

5. The evaluation of the learning or academic performance.

Educational psychology examines all those factors and their relationship with the academic performance of students.

A psycho-educational assessment is an analysis of the factors that are affecting the learning, retention, and academic performance of students. When all the factors listed above are included in the analysis, your child's uniqueness will be revealed. This is of utmost importance as it will provide (a) a guide to how you and the teacher should teach your child (b) child's abilities, and capabilities, that which he or she has the ability to do if taught how to do it, (c) experiences from birth up to the point of the assessment, (d) the dominant style of learning, and any physical or intellectual challenges. All are combined to create the learning profile which is a picture of the learner.

Academic underperformance is a "situation in which a bright child cannot or will not perform at an academic level commensurate with his or her intellectual ability" (Emerick, 1992). Children who underperform academically will exhibit certain behaviours and or attitudes towards their education.

To assist you in identifying whether or not your child is underperforming, I have provided the checklist below and in *Appendix C.*

Is Your Child Underperforming? Does He/She:

1. Fail to complete assignments/homework and has no interest in doing so or doing it well?

2. Score below the pass mark or standard set by the teacher/school?

3. Perform below or far below others in class?

4. Refuse to do schoolwork?

5. Often get report remarks like 'has the potential to do better'?

6. Have difficulty understanding, learning, remembering, or completing tasks?

Parents, are any of these scenarios familiar?

1. The teacher says your child can do better during consultation sessions.

2. The school calls you in to discuss your child's academic underperformance.

3. The child admits that more could have been done on a test/assignment/project.

4. Grades are lower than you expected, even if the grades are above the pass mark.

Other characteristics found in children who are underperforming academically are:

1. Knowing the answer but unable to write it well (communication deficit).

2. Poor performance in some subject areas and well in others.

3. Disorganized and/or poor study habits.

4. Gets easily frustrated and gives up trying when faced with challenges in the learning process.

5. Poor self-concept/self-esteem and low self-confidence.

6. Fear of failure or success (may not want to be referred to as a nerd).

7. Excessive need for attention/isolation.

8. Avoids responsibilities and competition.

9. Shares negative thoughts/has thoughts of being unintelligent despite getting good test results.

10. Confesses feelings of being unable to succeed despite high levels of intelligence.

Increasing Learning and Retention

The process of learning looks at the nature of learning and how it takes place. It looks at the principles and theories of learning, remembering, forgetting, understanding, thinking, reasoning, problem-solving, the transfer of knowledge, ways and means of effective learning etc. According to Kang (2019), there are five research-backed study techniques that will assist your child in learning what is being taught and retaining that knowledge for future use. They are:

1. *Pre-test:* Research has shown that pre-testing improves post-test results more than spending the same amount of time studying.

2. *Spacing out study sessions:* This involves focusing on a topic for a short period on different days. Creating flashcards that can be used for spaced practice and self-quizzing is effective. Students should create different piles when reviewing the flashcards. The cards they're able to answer immediately should be placed in a pile to review three days later; those answered with some difficulty should be reviewed two days later, and those that they answered incorrectly should be reviewed the next day.

3. *Self-quizzing:* Encourage students to make test questions for themselves as they learn a new concept, thinking about the types of questions you might ask on a quiz or test. They should incorporate these quizzes into

their study sessions, answering every question, even those they believe they know well.

4. *Interleaving practice*: An effective method of studying is to work on a set of problems that are related but not all of the same kind—for example, a set of math word problems that call for addition, subtraction, multiplication, or division. The consecutive problems cannot be solved with the same strategy.

5. *Paraphrasing and reflecting*: Utilize intentional learning strategies. These include relating what is being learned to prior knowledge, thinking about how they would explain the content, and reflecting on and asking questions about the content."

You may consult *Appendix D* for a detailed explanation of the strategies.

The learning environment refers to the physical conditions under which teaching or learning takes place: the temperature of the room or facility in which teaching or learning is taking place, group dynamics and the techniques or strategies being used to transfer the knowledge that the child is expected to grasp.

The teacher also plays a critical role in the learning process. The personality, attitude, aptitude, and knowledge of the teacher determine his or her ability to teach and effectively manage the classroom and student interactions and learning. The strategies that the teacher uses to teach a particular concept or idea must be appropriate and compatible with the student's age, developmental stage and learning style.

Evaluating Performance

The evaluation of the learning or academic performance of a child looks at how learning is evaluated, measured, or assessed. The tool used to assess if learning has taken place needs to be appropriate. The assessment instrument may be oral, performance-based or written. It can also be a combination of any or all the different methods. The conditions under which the assessment takes place is also important. Many students fear examinations and the conditions in which they are held; because silence is usually required and the expectations are often higher than that which is required for an in-class review of a lesson that has been taught.

School Reports and Their Role in Revealing Academic Challenges

Within most educational institutions, students are provided with reports on their performance at the end of a term and or the academic year. These reports reveal the level of the student's performance over the period assessed. Some of these reports focus only on the academic performance of students, while others include the attitudes, aptitude and conduct they displayed. A child whose report reveals a consistent level of underperformance needs attention and academic support. As parents, we need to pay very close attention to what is included in each report. The reports provide clues that can help parents to know the areas or subjects in which their children are struggling. As you examine your child's reports, look for patterns. Are there specific subjects or aspects of each subject that are consistently showing that the child is experiencing difficulty? Look at the profile for Mathematics, is Computation a problem, is Comprehension of the mathematical concepts proving to be a challenge? Examine the grades for English Language. Is Comprehension showing up as a challenge there too? Is Pronunciation a challenge? If it is, the child will find it difficult to spell and may underperform in several subjects.

Parent/Teacher Collaboration

Parents who get psycho-educational/psycho-social assessments for their children need to inform the school of the results of those assessments. This means sharing the results of the assessment, the diagnosis, and the recommendations to correct incidences of underperformance. If the evaluation reveals that the child has a learning disability or is academically challenged in specific subject areas, this must also be shared with the school.

In some instances, the school may make the arrangements to have the assessments conducted. When this approach is used, the school needs to ensure that the results are communicated and explained to the parents. Both the school and parents need to be reminded that:

• Two-way positive communication between home and school positively affects students' academic performance.

• When teachers use relevant means of communication to inform parents about school programmes and students' progress, parents will feel comfortable in contacting schools about their children's school life.

Stakeholders within the education sector are aware that the type of community in which a child lives, poverty, parents, the quality of their education and the school culture in teaching and learning, are factors that affect students' academic progress.

"How do I fix this?" you may ask. My response is that you make an appointment to discuss your concerns with the specific teacher(s) of the subject(s) about which you have concerns. Ask the teachers what strategies are being used to teach the child, then based on your knowledge of how the child learns best, suggest other strategies that may be explored by the teacher. You will also need to discuss all the other factors that affect the learning process with the teachers. Is the child attentive in class? Is he/she having a good relationship with the teacher? Is he/she afraid of tests? etc. At the end of those meetings, both you and the teacher should leave the meeting with a new or amended plan of how to fix the problems identified.

If the problems persist after the amended strategies are implemented over a time, you may need to get a tutor for your child. Finding a tutor who is trained to build the fundamental skills, identify the specific challenge being encountered in grasping the concepts, and patiently work with the child to correct the situation, is an important next step in improving that child's academic performance. As you seek to solve the problem, you may discover that it is more complicated than you and/or the teacher thought.

If that happens seek the assistance of a psychologist in resolving this challenge. A psychologist is trained to identify the specific challenges being encountered, develop a plan for having them resolved, and guide you through the process of change. It may also be recommended that you have the child medically examined to determine if there are physical challenges that are affecting the child's ability to learn. A child's ability to see and hear well is critical to the learning process.

In addition to the factors mentioned above, the psycho-educational assessment I conduct with parents and their children include what happens at home and other factors such as the parent-child relationship, family dynamics and the home environment. If the home does not provide a quiet, relaxed, and supportive environment, learning and the retention of what is being learnt will be difficult, if not impossible.

The principle of the home, school and child coming together to produce the educational outcome desired by all is very important. Many parents forget their role and that of the family in creating student success. Let's now turn our attention to how to support learning at home.

Chapter 4
Supporting Learning at Home

In this chapter, we'll explore how you can create a positive learning environment for your child at home. You will:

• Understand your child's true potential and gauge expectations.

• Learn how to give home support at the primary, high school and tertiary levels.

I was deeply troubled as I assisted a family member who was experiencing academic underperformance, but I chose to remain calm as I provided the necessary encouragement. I knew that if I joined everyone in bemoaning his low test results, he would sink into depression. I reflected on the strategies that I had learnt in dealing with such challenges as I sought to help him.

The family employed a tutor for Mathematics, used the time spent en route between school and home to revise his schoolwork and encouraged him to talk when he had performance doubts. He was also provided with pastoral counselling and medical support when needed. Both visits ended up as sessions of encouragement as both professionals motivated him to strive for academic excellence.

As I conducted further research on the phenomenon of academic underperformance, I discovered the following quotations from Bronfenbrenner (1979, p. 24) which provided much support.

> Students perform better in their schoolwork when they get adequate parental support at home.

Students need their parents to be involved in their education because they need to be controlled and monitored in their homework, schoolwork and getting private tutoring when necessary.

When parents are involved, students' behaviours are recorded as more positive and productive in nature.

Parents may motivate and build their children's self-esteem to support them in their school-work by:

- monitoring their homework
- visiting their school
- attending parent-teacher meetings
- supporting other school activities
- arranging for a private tutor for support when necessary
- providing support during examination periods
- managing assignment completion and timely submission
- keeping children motivated when discouragement sets in
- collaborating with the school to prevent or solve problems identified
- getting the necessary resources - textbooks, workbooks, data, Wi-Fi, class schedules on tv, newspaper

supplements, etc.

• creating or assisting in creating a daily or weekly schedule

• assist when you can or get help

• being supportive of the educational system, that is, establishing the rules and guidelines.

Research (Emerick, 1992) has shown that the following factors are important in improving academic achievement: (a) parental support of extracurricular activities, (b) parents, (c) the class, (d) goals associated with grades, (e) the teacher, and (f) the child. Parents need to balance work, parenting and the educational support needed by their child at home in order to reverse academic underperformance.

Understanding Your Child's True Potential – Gauging Expectations

Adrian's parents were distraught. He was not placed in any of his schools of choice, but at one within a volatile inner-city community. Though the school was in close proximity to the primary school he had attended; it was far from home. His parents questioned the placement of their son, despite the fact that all of the schools they selected as "schools of choice" only accepted students with averages above that which their son obtained during the Primary Exit Profile (PEP) examination. It was explained that although Adrian mastered all of his Grade Four Literacy tests and did well in the Performance-Based Examination in grade 5, it was in grade 6 that he began to excel. They were concerned that their son, who was of a quiet disposition, would have difficulty coping at the school at which he was placed.

Adrian may be considered a late bloomer, but he also had an affinity for the technical subjects, unlike his older brother and his younger sister. His parents, therefore, sought to have him transferred to another technical high school where they believed he would excel.

The case above demonstrates clearly what happens when parents overestimate their children's academic abilities, despite what is written on school reports, the children's uniqueness and natural abilities. Get to know your children. When we are aware of their strengths and weaknesses, use that information to make decisions that will be in their best interest. We cannot afford to allow pride or the opinions of others to influence our decisions. A child who is academically endowed must be encouraged to pursue academics and a child who is technically talented must be directed towards his/her area of gifting.

HOME SUPPORT

Marie is a Jamaican single parent. She has four children: one in university, two in high school and one in preparatory school. She is a self-employed professional and is very active in the civil organizations within her community and all the parent teachers' associations of the schools that her younger children attend. The two youngest children struggle academically. Their school fees are usually late and they do not have the resources they need to thrive at school. Despite her best efforts, Marie is failing at monitoring all their various class work, assignments and school supplies.

As parents, we have a responsibility to support the learning process at home. The types and levels of support provided may be directly connected to the educational level of each child. The current COVID-19 Pandemic which has resulted in the homeschooling of children globally has revealed the critical role of home-based parental support in the academic success of students. The following are specific recommendations for parents in supporting learning at home.

Primary School Level

Students should:

- have a private space for school activities
- be fed before class
- be settled and ready to learn at least 5 minutes before sessions
- follow a timetable or create a guide tailored to his/her pace
- organize tools needed for the day's task
- have a schedule: morning and afternoon with appropriate breaks
- be supervised
- store and organize their work safely in file folders.

High School Level

- Communicate the reasons for online sessions if classes are held via that medium
- Encourage your child to review 3 - 4 subjects daily: 1-1/2 hour time slots and note-taking.
- Encourage your child to read, review and practice past papers.

- Familiarize yourself with the CSEC and other external examination websites.

- Encourage your child to use multiple credible sources to research topics.

- Focus on understanding the concepts taught in each lesson.

- Be flexible: children can become stressed.

- Observe your child to determine changes in behavior in relation to schoolwork.

- Incorporate fun activities in your child's daily schedules - Chess, Hopscotch.

- Reward your child for progress made using stickers and other ideas shown below:

- Cake, ice cream, cookouts

- Praise
- Give them a Hi 5
- Do a victory dance
- Treats- candy, fruits, pastry
- Stay up late
- Puzzles
- Hugs and kisses

As you support your child's education emotionally and physically remember that they may need additional educational supplies that would usually be available at school. These tools may include:

- A printer and ink cartridges
- Printing Paper
- Stapler/staples
- Paper punch machine & fasteners
- Rubber bands
- File Folders
- Folder & folder leaves
- Scissors and cartridge paper
- Access to Wi-Fi and computer-based applications such as:
- Edmodo, Zoom, Google Classroom and YouTube

Rose's Story

Rose is a grade 11 student who is completing her School-Based-Assessments (SBAs). She was asked to lead the groups to complete the assignments. Despite the challenge of getting the different SBA groups to work seamlessly, all except one ended well. The interesting thing though is that the SBA that was not completed when she sought her mother's assistance would have affected the grades of two of her subjects (Principles of Accounts and Principles of Business). Days before the deadline for submission and after trying different ways to get all the members of the group to work together without success, she decided to do the entire project alone. Her mother, who was aware of some of the challenges that Rose had shared, cleared her schedule and decided to assist her. They worked as a team and Rose was able to submit the SBA on time.

Both the Caribbean Examination Council (CXC) and the Ministry of Education, Jamaica (which administers the former Grade Six Achievement Test (GSAT), now the Primary Exit Profile (PEP)) - the two major external examination bodies that prepare testing mechanisms for Jamaican children to exit the primary and secondary education sectors, have sought to expand the strategies used to assess student learning. The two exit examination systems have added performance task-oriented examinations known as School-Based Assessments (SBAs) in addition to the series of in-school/site final examinations for the various subjects offered.

A major aim of this exercise is to provide multiple opportunities for the students to demonstrate mastery of the concepts they have learnt and provide opportunities for students with varying learning styles to learn and demonstrate their knowledge of the concepts taught. While the assignments are challenging enough for the students, an explicit objective built into the process is the inclusion of parental or other adult support to guarantee the successful completion of projects assigned or chosen by the students.

While many parents understand and accept this responsibility, others cower in fear and do very little to help their children. This form of parental neglect has caused many academically competent children to develop low self-esteem and perform way below their abilities.

The practice of supporting one's child has to continue beyond the early childhood level, where assignments that are obviously beyond the child's ability to achieve on his/her own call for parental or adult involvement, can be completed collaboratively. Many parents have expressed frustration as their attempts at helping their children at the primary level with assignments were met with resistance whenever they contradicted the approaches being used by their children's teachers. Some have given up and in frustration allowed their children to figure things out on their own.

This abandonment of parental support has sometimes resulted in learning gaps and missed opportunities to connect the dots among the different subject areas. Children fail to develop the skill of collaborative learning and often struggle on their own to meet school requirements. The results? Failing students and frustrated parents.

Tertiary Level

Some parents do not believe that their children who are enrolled in tertiary institutions need support at home. Although many of these students are adults, be mindful of the following:

• They need to be provided with all the resources they need to succeed in school.

- Many need a personal computer/laptop to prepare and submit the digital documents their school requires.

- They will also get stressed and discouraged and will need their parents' emotional support.

- It is extremely important that students at the tertiary level be provided with the financial support that they require to pay their tuition and other administrative and school-related expenses.

- Tertiary students, like other students who were forced to study online, will need reliable online support.

- This will include a reliable internet connection, a quiet home environment and freedom from chores during school hours.

Failure to provide these resources may result in the underperformance of academically capable students.

Summary

Regardless of the educational level, smart children and young adults may underperform. The key is to understand the factors that are contributing to academic underperformance and implement measures to correct the situation.

Research has shown that academic achievement may be improved if children perceive that their parents have a positive expectation of their academic performance. The data has shown that parental impact may be primarily of a psychological nature and relates to the students' feelings of self-worth.

Moon (2004) found in a study conducted on improving academic achievement that "students perceived that their parents contributed to their academic success in three ways:

1. The parents had directly or indirectly approved of and supported the children's out-of-school interests. In general, the students' regarded this support as an indication that their parents valued them for more than their achievements in school.

2. The students indicated that their parents had maintained a positive attitude toward them, even in the face of academic failure.

3. The students also believed the parents had eventually placed the responsibility for performance in school directly on them" (Moon (p.111-112).

A major takeaway from that study is the critical role that parents play and must continue to play in the lives of children who are underperforming academically. Let us allow them to have fun and live balanced lives while they are in school and be patient and supportive if or whenever they fall behind. We must also empower them to do whatever it takes to excel in school while being assured of our unconditional love and support.

Chapter 5
Preparing Your Child for External/Final Exams

In this chapter, we will explore various requirements or expectations of the institutions and examiners involved in the assessment of our children's academic performance. The specific topics to be covered are:

- External Examinations – Assessment criteria

- PEP

- CSEC/CAPE
- Bachelor's, Master's and Doctoral degree theses/dissertations
- Appendices: Institutional Resources - links to websites

E ducation is expensive, but the rewards are great! As parents, we need to invest in the educational development of our children. This will involve planning for each stage of their academic career. Each academic institution has its own system of academic assessment, designed to ascertain the extent of students' performance. Countries also have various systems for the external assessment of students as they seek to establish benchmarks of academic performance.

Let's examine a few of the systems of external assessment in Jamaica, the country in which the book was written.

The Primary Exit Profile (PEP)

PEP is a national external examination system designed to assess the academic performance of Jamaican children as they prepare for exiting the primary level of education. It is broken down into three major examinations which are given to students in Grades 4, 5 and 6 respectively.

What every parent needs to know:

- The Ministry of Education's PEP website (pep.moey.gov.jm) and the resources available there (MOEY, 2019).

- The subjects that will be tested at each grade and stage.

- The types of assessments and what each entails.

- What the student needs to accomplish to successfully complete each requirement (these are different for each area being assessed).

- PEP requirements – consult each subject syllabus.

- The PEP Exam Calendar and what will be examined at each grade and stage.

- Know where to go for assistance – know where to go and how to identify when it is needed.

- Locate and acquire reference/library materials and other items needed to complete each project.

As parents, you must also:

- Review, proofread and edit assignments before submission deadlines.

- Request Progress Report/Recommendations for improvement from each teacher.

- Help your child to make the recommended changes/improvements.

- Get help if the process is challenging and you do not know what to do.

- Learn to interpret the results (PEP Scores).

- Seek to understand how school placement is determined.

- Prepare your children to bloom wherever they are planted.

The Caribbean Secondary Education Certificate (CSEC)

C SEC is a regional examination administered by the Caribbean Examinations Council (CXC). The exams are available to students in the Caribbean at the secondary level. One of the components of the CSEC exam is the completion of School-Based-Assessments (SBAs). This assessment represents the performance-based element and requires collaboration for completion. While some SBAs may be done individually, many are done in groups where students are taught how to work collaboratively.

This assessment type, though designed to ensure the comprehensive testing of the candidates, has brought untold challenges and frustrations for the students, teachers, and parents. As with other assignments, group work that demands cooperation from each member of the team can be frustrating. Some students do not complete their respective assignments and may not communicate the reason for this negligence as in the case of Rose mentioned earlier.

Due to the significance of the projects, parents are forced to intervene in order to guarantee academic success. I advocated for parental involvement in the SBA completion process, having heard the cries of the students, teachers, and parents.

Caribbean Advanced Proficiency Examination (CAPE)

CAPE is also a regional examination administered by the Caribbean Examinations Council (CXC). The exams are available to students in the Caribbean at the upper secondary level. One of the components of the CAPE exam is the completion of Internal Assessments (IAs). This assessment represents the performance-based element and requires a significant amount of student-teacher collaboration for completion. While some IAs may be done individually, some are done in groups where students are taught how to work collaboratively.

Guide for SBAs and IAs for CSEC and CAPE

Parents must acquire the tools needed to supervise their children in completing their school-based assessments. The resources and instructions may be found at https://www.cxc.org/.

Here is a guide to your child's completion of the SBAs and IAs.

• Create an account or sign in if you already did. You will need an email address and password.

• Go to My Account to download the eBook to your laptop, tablet, or desktop computer.

• The process is similar for past papers except that you must add billing information to pay for them.

As a parent you need to know:

• The subjects that require an SBA: not all CSEC subjects do.

• What the student needs to do in order to complete each SBA successfully: requirements are different for each one.

• CXC's requirements for CSEC and CAPE. Consult the subject syllabus at https://www.cxc.org.

• Major milestones and submission date(s) - Concept Paper/Proposal/Research Report.

- Where to go and how to identify, locate and acquire reference/library materials and other items needed to complete each project.

As a parent, you must also:

- Periodically review the work completed before the submission deadlines.

- Request Progress Report/Recommendations for improvement from each teacher.

- Help your child to make the recommended changes.

- Proofread and edit each milestone document prior to submission.

- Get help if the process is challenging and you do not know what to do.

The Tertiary Level Institutional Requirements

Bachelor's/Master's/Doctoral Degree Theses/Dissertations
I supervise the final research papers of students at the master's and doctoral levels. The experience has opened my eyes to the various nuisances within various institutions regarding the format of the final theses/dissertations. While the general framework remains the same, the stages within the process, the number of chapters and the contents within each chapter sometimes vary.

Knowing the specific requirements of each institution will greatly reduce the frustration already embedded within the research process. The other factor that will greatly influence the students' progress and the timeliness of the achievement of the various milestones is the presence of and types of systems that the institution has in place to facilitate the successful completion of this programme's requirement for its students.

Quality control systems and checks are extremely important within the research process. However, while some institutions have institutional review boards/ethical committees, others do not. Notwithstanding, the key is to find out what the requirements are, the resources that are available to help the students and where or to whom you should go for help. The Nova Southeastern University's Centre for Collaborative Research was my main source of support as I completed my doctoral dissertation. Does the institution in which your child is enrolled have a similar website for research support?

Depending on the result of this search you may need external assistance. There are a number of specialized resources available with varying degrees of support. The key is to know the type of support that is needed and where to get it. Do not be tempted to pay anyone to do the intellectual work that your child needs to do for himself/herself. This constitutes intellectual fraud and may result in expulsion from the institution. Above all, such fraudulent behaviour robs the student of the opportunities for growth and development intellectually, academically and otherwise which should have been the purpose for the studies in the first place.

Chapter 6

Reversing Academic Underperformance

In this chapter we will:

• Examine how to eliminate learning gaps such as those arising from the COVID-19 pandemic.

• Explore the use of school reports in identifying concerns arising from trends and patterns that may not have been identified or acknowledged.

• Reinforce the need to get the foundation right to prevent problems at other levels of the education system.

COVID-19 Learning Gaps and Solutions

The COVID-19 pandemic forced the closure of all schools and triggered an immediate dependence on parents to support online learning and schooling. This revealed the need to include parents in the teaching and learning process. Parents were called upon to ensure that their children got appropriate devices, internet connectivity and attended classes wirelessly. While some parents succeeded in supporting their children, others gave up in frustration with the technology, the inability of school administrations to pivot quickly, inadequate financial resources and the inability to stay home to monitor their minor children.

The ancient African proverb, 'it takes a village to raise a child,' became a reality. Due to the communicable nature of the COVID-19 virus and the protocols developed to slow and eventually eliminate its transmission, many students found themselves at home and cut off from school. That resulted in the creation of learning gaps and the search for solutions to provide students with access to classes that were being held online. The "village" was called upon to provide support services to parents in bridging the learning gaps. As a parent and an executive member of a regional parent teachers' association, I joined with a few colleagues and published in the news media several strategies that parents could employ to bridge those learning gaps. Most of them have been included here for your information.

What should you do if your child has fallen behind academically?

1. *Assess Your Situation in Relation to the Threat*

Be courageous. Parents all over the world are having similar problems. You are not alone and help is available. Our educational administrators, while dealing with their own fears, have developed various strategies to deal with the anticipated effects of the pandemic. Among the strategies shared is the assessment of our children to ascertain the learning gaps that were expected due to the sudden transition to online learning. If your child has fallen behind, don't panic. Accept the fact, seek advice on how to fix the problem and act immediately.

2. *Get Help for Your Child*

I have spoken to many parents who got frustrated and gave up the fight for their children's right to a good education. My advice to those parents continues to be "If at first you don't succeed, try again another way". The lessons on resilience that you have learnt and seek to teach your children must now be put in practice. Learn about and use the protocols in place within the education system to get help for your child.

• Contact your child's teachers and share your concerns. If they are uncooperative, contact a supervisor.

• If you get no results or only receive a part of the solution you seek, go higher.

• If the school is not responsive, contact the Ministry of Education's Regional Office.

• If they fail, contact the Head Office.

Your child's future is too important to be abandoned. Seek out every opportunity to get all the help you need.

3. Respond to the Strategies Being Implemented by Schools in Response to the Pandemic

You need to develop a Family Response Plan. This will involve an understanding of the measures being implemented at the school. Think of ways in which each member of the family can work together to achieve their various goals. Will your child be expected to stay at home some days? How do you plan to ensure that assignments are done and that he or she is safely supervised while you are at work?

Attend PTA sessions organized to teach parents how to respond/cope with the changes while staying on the right side of the law. Child neglect is a form of child abuse and cannot be tolerated.

Is there a relative, neighbour, friend, or church sister/brother who you can trust to assist with schoolwork? Is there a childcare centre close to your home or workplace? Is there a library nearby? Can your workplace provide support? Think community, and while you do, think safety.

If your child is expected to continue school online, you will need a reliable internet connection. This will allow your child to seamlessly access all the sessions, download apps and submit assignments. If you don't have an internet connection then one option is to discuss with your Internet Service Provider (ISP) what internet service would best meet your child's needs and fit within your budget.

Get a printer and laptop or tablet for your child. Smartphones will not be able to effectively fulfil school requirements. These are costly items. Support the National Parent Teachers' Association as it lobbies for the removal of Custom duties and other taxes associated with the importation/purchase of these items. If you are faced with a severe financial need, find out how to access government and special interest group programmes of assistance.

Identify or create safe community spaces and centres for children to access WIFI and do their assignments.

Carpool and participate in pooled childcare and pickup services.

If you are in need, find out about care packages being provided by PTAs and other entities. They may include back to school supplies.

Find out how the church you attend can assist students who will be asked to stay at home or work remotely without the necessary resources.

Recommend that the church host extra classes in their halls or worship centres.

If your church has a tent, recommend that it rents/lends it to schools that need extra classroom spaces?

Recommend that the unemployed/underemployed youths in your congregation tutor/supervise those still in school.

Submit your name for the development of a community-based database with skills that can be employed to provide an income for families which are affected by layoffs and unemployment.

Access psychological support services if you are struggling to cope with the proposed changes in the educational system.

Remember, we have the option to sit and complain, to panic and cast blame or to embrace the African proverb that "It takes a village to raise a child".

Let's be wise and be guided by Dale Carnegie who stated that inaction breeds doubt and fear. Action breeds confidence and courage. If you want to conquer fear, do not sit home, and think about it. Go out and get busy.

Home-Based Support and Academic Success

A psychologist is trained to identify the specific challenges being encountered, develop a plan for having them resolved, and guide the parent/guardian and child through the process of change. During the psycho-educational assessment conducted with you, the parents/guardians and the child, what happens at home and other factors such as the parent-child relationship, family dynamics and the home environment will be discussed.

If the home does not provide a quiet, relaxed, and supportive environment, learning and the retention of what is being learnt will be difficult, if not impossible. The principle of the home, school and child working together to produce the educational outcome desired by all, will become evident. Do not forget your role and that of the family in creating student success.

The current COVID-19 Pandemic which resulted in the homeschooling of children globally revealed the critical role of home-based parental support in the academic success of students. The following factors are important in improving academic achievement: (a) out-of-school interests/activities, (b) parents, (c) goals associated with grades and (d) the child.

Parents are expected to support the learning process at home. The types and levels of support provided at home may be directly connected to the educational level of each child.

The following are specific recommendations for supporting learning at home:

At the Primary Level

- Create a private space for your child.

- Feed your child before class.

- Ensure that your child is settled and ready to learn at least 5 minutes before the session begins.

- Follow a timetable or create a guide tailored to your child's pace.

- Organize tools needed for the day's task.

- Have a schedule: morning and afternoon with appropriate breaks.

- Try to supervise your child.

- Teach your child to store his/her work safely.

- Help your child to organize their work in file folders.

The practice of supporting one's child has to continue beyond the early childhood level, where assignments, which are obviously beyond the child's ability and which called for parental or adult involvement, are completed collaboratively. Many parents have expressed frustration as their attempts at helping their children at the primary level with assignments were met with resistance whenever they contradict the approaches being used by their children's teachers. Some have given up and in frustration have allowed their children to figure things out on their own.

This abandonment of parental support has resulted in learning gaps and missed opportunities to connect the dots among the different subject areas. Children fail to develop the skill of collaborative learning and often struggle on their own to meet school requirements. The results? Failing students and frustrated parents.

At the Secondary Level

- Communicate with your child regarding the reasons for the online sessions.

- Encourage the child to review 3 to 4 subjects each day: 1-1/2 time slots and take notes, using a pen.

- Encourage your child to read, review and practice past papers, make use of the CSEC and other external examination websites and use credible sources to research topics.

- Ensure that your child understands the concepts taught in each lesson and is flexible: children can become stressed.

- Observe your child to determine changes in his/her behaviour in relation to schoolwork.

- Incorporate fun activities in their daily schedules - Chess, Hopscotch, family fun days.

- Reward your child.

At the Tertiary Level

Some parents do not believe that their children who are enrolled in tertiary institutions need support at home.

Although many of these students are adults -

• They need to be provided with all the resources they need to succeed in school.

• Many of them will be required to prepare and submit digital documents and will need a personal computer/laptop.

• They will also get stressed and discouraged and will need their parents' emotional support.

• It is extremely important that students at the tertiary level be provided with the financial support that they require to pay their tuition and other administrative and school-related expenses.

• Failure to provide these resources may result in the underperformance of academically capable students.

• Tertiary students, like other students who were forced to study online, will need reliable online support.

• This will include a reliable internet connection, a quiet home environment and freedom from chores during school hours.

Regardless of the educational level, smart children and young adults may underperform. The key is to understand the factors that are contributing to academic underperformance and implement measures to correct the situation. Research has shown that academic achievement may be improved if children perceive that their parents have positive expectations for their improved academic performance. The data has shown that parental impact may be primarily of a psychological nature and relates to the students' feelings of self-worth.

Coping with Learning Difficulties

If you are worried DON'T wait. If you suspect that your child's learning difficulties may require special assistance, please do not delay in finding support. The sooner you move forward, the better are your child's chances of reaching his or her full potential.

Medical Help

If your child is underperforming, get him/her medically examined to determine whether or not there are physical challenges that are affecting the ability to learn. I have heard many adults talk about the difficulties they encountered with regard to being able to see the chalkboard or hear the teacher while they were in school and how those experiences affected their ability to learn.

A child's ability to see and hear well is critical to the learning process. This is because they will not learn the concepts being taught and will later have difficulty recalling the information in preparation for their examinations. Among children with reading disabilities, classroom teachers have reported a relatively high prevalence of the signs of vision disorders including, facial grimacing, squinting, head tilting, eye rubbing and unusually close working distance. If a level of reading success is not achieved, the quality of life for the individual as well as society as a whole is diminished.

There are also other medical challenges that may affect a child's ability to attend school regularly or perform well while at school or home. Children afflicted with cancers, diabetes, mental illness, and other neurological conditions are often too ill to complete assignments and participate in examinations. In order to improve their academic performance, parents need to request accessibility support for students with physical or mental disabilities, including blindness, low vision, hearing impairments, mobility impairments, learning disabilities, and other health impairments.

This pandemic alerted many individuals to the psychology of learning and the relationship between one's psychological health and academic performance. The psychology of learning focuses on how people learn and interact with their environments. When children are fearful, anxious, or depressed they will have difficulty concentrating or grasping what is being taught. The fear of underachievement in both internal and external examinations which had the potential to determine their future plagued many children and their parents. Valiant efforts were therefore made to bridge the learning gaps that arose in the initial phase of the pandemic.

The other significant factor that affects the academic performance of thousands of children is the socioeconomic status of their families. Albert Bandura who developed the Social Learning Theory (1977) stated that learning takes place within a context and the learning environment affects a child's ability to learn, to retain that which is taught and to use the knowledge that has been gained. Students from families with the financial resources or connections to provide the necessary learning resources were able to resume classes as soon as online schooling began. Many schools which insisted on the need to keep video cameras on had to abandon the practice, as the varying home environments, fluctuating WiFi connectivity and distractions within the homes, made class control more challenging for teachers.

As the transition to a hybrid or blended system of learning (face to face and online) takes place, poverty reduction will have to be prioritized to ensure that all children receive 'an equal opportunity to be educated' despite the challenges. Childhood poverty has negatively affected academic performance and will necessitate the involvement of the village to reverse the situation. It is critical that parents who are struggling to feed their children and provide the resources needed to ensure academic success seek support from persons within their extended families and communities.

School Reports

In this section, you will learn how to use your child's school report to pinpoint learning gaps and challenges. For this activity, gather all the reports you have ever received for your child from as early as pre-school.

Organize them from oldest to newest, examining each section of the reports.

Early Childhood/Day Care Level

Look carefully at the developmental milestones assessed and the teachers'/caregivers' general evaluation of your child's emotional, behavioural, and cognitive/thinking skills.

Kindergarten/Basic/Infant School Level

Scrutinize the developmental milestones assessed and the teachers'/caregivers' general evaluation of your child's emotional, behavioural, and cognitive/thinking skills. Are there any difficulties or challenges highlighted? Reflect on what is shared and whether you were aware of them. Were recommendations provided to correct/manage or resolve the challenges?

Did you or can you do anything to solve those challenges? If you did, did you get the results anticipated? If you did not, is it too late now?

Preparatory/Primary/Elementary Level

Examine the grades given for each subject. Are there sub-categories under each? For example, Mathematics is segmented into Comprehension/Understanding and Computation/Calculation. Was mastery attained in all areas? Highlight any area of concern? Were the areas of concern addressed? Were recommendations made on how to correct the problems identified? What has been done and did the actions taken to bring the expected results? If nothing was done, will correcting that problem solve others? e.g., For instance; if your son/daughter has not mastered the skill of reading, that problem will affect their ability to understand instructions given in all other subjects. Get help immediately from the teachers and if possible, employ tutors to deal with the specific challenges identified. Bridge the gaps identified now to prevent the problems from worsening later.

High/Secondary School Level

Analyze the grades given for each subject, repeating the steps employed at the primary/preparatory level but with greater fervency. Your child is now approaching the teen years. Comprehension skills are paramount at this level. Any deficiency will affect his/her ability to understand instructions given in all other subjects; and therefore the ability to do those subjects well. Research the specific requirements for each of the subjects for which your child will be externally examined.

If at the end of the secondary level your child plans to pursue studies at the tertiary level, examine closely the grades that he/she received for each subject taken during the latter years of high school and in external examinations. Look at the profiles for each subject taken in external examinations, look at Mathematics, for example. Was mastery achieved in the areas of Comprehension/Calculation? Did your child master all subjects/areas? Are there areas of concern? Are they being addressed? Were attempts made to address them? Were recommendations made on how to correct the problems identified?

What has been done and did those actions bring the expected results? If nothing was done, will correcting that problem solve others? For example, if he/she has not mastered the skill of Computation or subjects in the Sciences/Arts/Business field(s), that problem will affect his/her ability to excel in related subjects; and therefore, the ability to do those subjects well. This is your final opportunity to get it right. Therefore, if your child did not matriculate to the tertiary sector and still has a keen interest in furthering their education, get help from subject experts, and if possible, employ tutors to deal with the specific challenges.

Within the Caribbean, some institutions will allow students to repeat the final year. Take advantage of this facility if it is available. If no such facility exists, get assistance from the school in identifying alternate ways of bridging the gap between high school and college or university.

At the Tertiary Level

Do not assume that because your child has been accepted in a tertiary institution that all learning gaps identified earlier were either corrected or managed. Students at the tertiary level also struggle and may have carried with them phobias that may affect their academic achievement. One of the most common examples identified at one of the universities in which I worked was that some students would fail Calculus repeatedly due to a fear of Mathematics that was not previously addressed. Once your child becomes an adult, the institution cannot release his/her report to you without the student's consent and school reports are not sent to parents as their responsibility for the student would have legally ended.

At this level, you will need to change your parenting style and approach in order to support your child's academic journey. Assure him/her of your continued commitment to his/her academic success and your willingness to assist if problems arise and they need your help. Teach them how to identify and resolve academic challenges as soon as they arise and to inform you if they need help in getting them resolved. Talk with them often, keep checking on them, unless they express annoyance and ask for less help. Build or maintain good communication with them and ask about their assignments and exams and get updates on their grades at the end of each academic term.

Teach them how to monitor their grades and grade point average (GPA) as this will affect the type of degree that they will be awarded. Loosen the reins as they complete their first year in college or university and continue to monitor from a distance their academic performance.

"A stitch in time saves nine"

The idea behind conducting a detailed analysis of your child's past and present educational challenges is to identify the specific areas of concern. Knowing what can be done, like identifying the resources needed to fix them (tools, people, approaches etc.) is half the battle. It is critical that problems identified are fixed or managed. If they are not, the foundation for learning would be less than ideal.

This approach is supported by the principle of getting it right from the early childhood level. Just as a building with a faulty foundation will crumble, so is a child's education that is shaky or has gaps at the pre-primary, primary and high school levels. The lament at tertiary institutions in Jamaica and other countries continues to be a lack of suitably qualified applicants/matriculants.

Many institutions have had to introduce remedial programmes to equip their students to perform at the required standards. Advise your child to utilize all support services established by his/her institution to bridge the gaps and to address any social or psychological challenge that may result from them failing a subject. Teach them how to learn from failures and to prevent them from recurring.

Any child who has not developed the right combination of cognitive abilities/skills, will have great difficulty moving from one level of the education system to the next. As a country, Jamaica cannot afford to have less than half of its high school graduates matriculating to the tertiary level because of academic underperformance (MOEYI, 2021). As parents, the responsibility is ours to ensure that our children receive the best foundation that they need to fulfil their career dreams.

Chapter 7
Learning Disabilities and Academic Underperformance

In this chapter, we will examine learning disabilities and what to do to assist your child. The areas to be covered include:

- Learning disabilities/challenges
- What to do and how to help your child

In this section, I will focus on common learning disabilities. The content was prepared by a team of special educators. It contains important tips on (1) the signs and symptoms of learning disabilities, (2) what to do if you suspect that your child may have a learning disability, (3) the team of professionals available to help you cope with such a diagnosis and (4) the support systems available to ensure that your child performs at his/her best. The title of this book, *It Still Takes a Village*, will be further demonstrated as you understand that learning disabilities will affect academic underperformance, but help is available.

Hammil, Leigh, McNutt & Larsen (1988) defines learning disabilities as a heterogeneous group of disorders manifested by significant difficulties in the acquisition and use of listening, speaking, reading, writing, reasoning or mathematical abilities. These disorders are intrinsic to the individual and presumed to be due to Central Nervous System Dysfunction. A learning disability is also defined as "any mental condition that prevents a person from acquiring the same amount of knowledge as others in their age group."

My first encounter with a learning disability came a few years ago when a friend expressed the concern that her son refused to write in school and that his grades, though good, could have been better if he completed assignments given. There was nothing medically wrong with him, he just did not want to write. Today, his parents are in a better place, as the employment of a special educator and plans to provide this necessary support at school, bring hope that he will maximize his potential.

What can you do?

It can be difficult to face the possibility that your child has a learning disorder. No parent wants to see his or her child suffer. You may wonder what it could mean for your children's future or worry about how they will make it through school. Perhaps you're concerned that they might be labelled "slow" or assigned to a remedial class.

The earlier we detect learning difficulties the better it is for your child. There are strategies that can be employed collaboratively to ensure the success of your child.

Signs and Symptoms

Learning disabilities are problems that affect the brain's ability to receive, process, analyze, or store information. These problems can make it difficult for a student to learn as quickly as someone who isn't affected by learning disabilities.

Learning disabilities may manifest themselves in one or a combination of the areas of learning and challenges/problems listed below:

- reading and/or writing

- math or computing

- memory deficits

- paying attention

- following directions

- clumsiness

- telling time

- staying organized

- acting without really thinking about possible outcomes (impulsiveness)• "Acting out" in school or social situations
- difficulty staying focused; being easily distracted
- difficulty saying a word correctly aloud or expressing thoughts
- problems with school performance from week to week or day-to-day
- speaking like a younger child; using short, simple phrases; or leaving out words in sentences
- having a hard time listening
- problems dealing with changes in schedule or situations
- problems understanding words or concepts.

The characteristics above may be manifested in any of the common learning disabilities listed below:

1. *Dysgraphia*

Dysgraphia can be related to the physical act of writing. While reading disabilities are more common, writing disabilities exist and are equally difficult to overcome. These students often cannot hold a pencil correctly, and their posture may be tense while trying to write. This leads them to tire easily, causing discouragement that further inhibits progress.

Dysgraphia can also refer to difficulty with written expression. These students have trouble organizing their thoughts coherently. Their writing may be redundant or have obvious omissions that affect the quality and readability of the text. Dysgraphia may also cause students to struggle with basic sentence structure and grammatical awareness.

2. *Dyslexia*

Dyslexia is perhaps the most known learning disability. It is a learning disorder that impedes the student's ability to read and comprehend a text. There are a variety of ways in which this disability can be manifested. Some persons struggle with phonemic awareness which is the ability to notice, think about, and work with the individual sounds in spoken words. They fail to recognize the way words break down according to sound. Such as isolating and saying the first and last sound in a word (e.g. the beginning sound of dog is "d" and the ending sound of sit is "t".) This often results in them using general use words like "thing" and "stuff" instead of the names of objects (Readingrockets.org, 2021).

Similar problems can occur with phonological processing, wherein students cannot distinguish between similar word sounds that rhyme such as cat, rat and fat. Other issues relate generally to fluency, spelling, comprehension, and computation. Students may experience one reading issue or multiple issues when struggling with dyslexia. Dyslexia impacts the child's ability to read, spell, write, and speak.

3. *Attention Deficit Hyperactivity Disorder (ADHD)*

Attention Deficit/Hyperactivity Disorder has affected many children at some point. While there is some debate as to whether or not ADHD is a learning disability in the most technical sense, there is no doubt that it is a common learning impediment. Students who have ADHD have difficulty paying attention and staying on task. These students can be easily distracted and often have difficulty in traditional school settings.

Experts link ADHD with the structure of the brain, and there is evidence that this condition may have a genetic component as well. Unlike typical learning disabilities, which need instructional interventions, ADHD can be successfully treated with medications and behavioural therapies.

4. *Processing Deficits*

Learning disabilities are also connected to processing deficits. When students have a processing deficit, they have trouble making sense of sensory data, such as what is heard or seen. This makes it hard for them to perform in a traditional classroom without instructional support.

These deficits are most often auditory or visual, and they can make it hard for students to distinguish and remember important information that is necessary for them to succeed.

5. *Dyscalculia*

Math is another major area of concern when it comes to learning disabilities. While difficulty with reading can affect a student's ability in math, some students also suffer from dyscalculia, which is a disorder that specifically affects one's math capabilities.

Dyscalculia can range from an inability to order numbers correctly and extend to limited strategies for problem-solving. Students with math disorders may have trouble performing basic math calculations, or they may have difficulty with concepts like time, measurement, or estimation.

6. *Impairment in Executive Functioning*

An impairment in executive functioning results in a cognitive disability that impacts a person's daily life. There is an inefficiency in the cognitive management systems of the brain. These skills are controlled by the brain's frontal lobe. It affects a wide variety of processes like strategizing, planning, paying attention to details, organization, remembering details, and managing time and space. Problems with executive functioning are almost always present among people who have ADHD or specific learning disabilities.

Below is information on autism as children on the spectrum may also experience learning difficulties.

7. *Autism*

Difficulty mastering certain academic skills can stem from pervasive developmental disorders such as Autism and Asperger's syndrome. Children with Autism spectrum disorders may have trouble communicating, reading body language, learning basic skills, making friends, and making eye contact.

These learning disabilities are the most common ones and can manifest with varying degrees of severity. Some children may struggle with multiple disabilities. By understanding them, it is possible to find workable solutions so that every child can thrive in the classroom, at home and in the future.

Help from Specialists

The following specialists are able to diagnose the presence of learning disabilities in children:

• Clinical, School Educational/ Developmental, Counselling Psychologists

• Child psychiatrists

• Neuropsychologist

• Psychometrist/Psychometrician (person who administers tests for specific academic challenges)

• Speech and language therapist

• Special Educators at the Ministry of Education Special Education Unit

Ministry of Education, Youth and Information (MOEYI) Special Education Unit offers:

- Shadow Services – If a child has a special need and cannot function on his/her own in the school setting, someone may be assigned to work with that child in school to help him/her access the curriculum.

- Placement of students who have been formally diagnosed to be in need of special educational support. The process involves an application to the Ministry's Special Education Unit. After the assessment report is reviewed, the child is placed in a school best suited to meet his/her needs. The Ministry has Memoranda of Understanding (MOUs) with some private schools to compensate for the shortage of spaces in public schools.

- The processing of assessment reports in order to provide special accommodations to students sitting external examinations such as PEP – Grades 4/5/6 and CSEC or CAPE.

- Screening services for students who are in need of formal assessment. This service is offered by the Regional Assessment Teams – available in some regions

- Continuous public awareness to update and inform the public about students with special needs and the resources available to help them.

- Parental consultation – offers suggestions to parents about the availability of services for children with special needs across the system.

These services are available directly from the Ministry's Head Office Special Education Unit and at Regional Offices (through Special Needs Coordinators). You may also consult *Appendix E - Directory of Services* for additional services and online resources available to support children with disabilities.

Best Practices for Parents

The following recommendations may be used by the parents of children who learn slowly or have learning disabilities:

• Learn the specifics about your child's learning disability. Read articles, listen, and watch audio and video presentations about your child's learning disability. Find out how the disability affects the learning process and what cognitive (thinking) skills are involved. It's easier to evaluate learning techniques if you understand how the learning disability affects your child.

• Research treatments, services, and new theories about the disability/disorder. Find out all you can about the type of learning disability your child has. Educate yourself about the most effective treatment options available. This can help you advocate for your child at school and pursue treatment at home.

• Pursue treatment and services at home. Even if the school doesn't have the resources to treat your child's learning disability optimally, you can pursue these options on your own at home or with a therapist or tutor.

• Nurture your child's strengths. Even though children with learning disabilities struggle in one area of learning, they may excel in another. Pay attention to your child's interests and passions. Helping children with learning disorders develop their passions and strengths will probably help them with the areas of difficulty as well.

Social and Emotional Skills:
How can you help?

Effects on the Child

Learning disabilities can be extremely frustrating for children. Imagine having trouble with a skill all of your friends are tackling with ease, worrying about embarrassing yourself in front of the class or struggling to express yourself. Things can be doubly frustrating for exceptionally bright children with learning disabilities—a scenario that's not uncommon.

Interpersonal Relationships

Children with learning disabilities may have trouble expressing their feelings, calming themselves down, and reading nonverbal cues from others. This can lead to difficulty in the classroom and with their peers. The good news is that, as a parent, you can have a huge impact in these areas.

Social and Emotional skills

Social and emotional skills are the most consistent indicators of success for all children—and that includes children with learning disorders. They outweigh everything else, including academic skills, in predicting lifelong achievement and happiness.

Psychosocial Effects

Learning disabilities, and their accompanying academic challenges, can lead to low self-esteem, isolation, and behaviour problems, but they don't have to.

Support Systems

You can counter these effects by creating a strong support system for children with learning disabilities and helping them learn to express themselves, deal with frustration, and work through challenges.

Focus on their strengths

By focusing on your child's growth as a person, and not just on academic achievements, you'll help them learn good emotional habits that set the stage for success throughout life.

Frustrations and Results

You may experience some frustration trying to work with your child, and it can seem like an uphill battle when you don't have the information you need. After you learn what their specific learning disability is and how it is affecting their behaviours, you will be able to start addressing the challenges in school and at home.

Support Groups

If you can, be sure to reach out to other parents who are dealing with similar challenges as they can be great sources of knowledge and emotional support.

Create a Support Group if none exists.

MOST IMPORTANTLY, Whatever you do, DO NOT GIVE UP ON YOUR CHILD.

Gifted Children Underperform Too

The concept of gifted children underperforming academically has baffled the minds of parents and educators globally. Many children who excel academically beyond their biological years, encounter challenges that prevent them from maximizing their true potentials. When seeking to support these children:

> It is important to identify the underachiever's areas of strength and talent. Personal interests can motivate the student to learn and provide an avenue for learning various skills related to school success. Providing an appropriately challenging curriculum during the period of underachievement also appears to be important. School personnel should consider gifted underachievers candidates for gifted education services and/or advanced classes. Gifted students who underperform academically may respond well to parents and teachers who have high expectations, so provide calm and consistent guidance, and maintain a positive, objective regard for the student. Rest assured that academic underachievement can be reversed with modifications on the part of both the student and the school (Emerick, 1992, pp. 146).

The following recommendations arose from a study concerning improving academic achievement in gifted children who underperform academically:

1. Parents of gifted underachievers are to be included in determining the educational needs of their children. The importance of parental support and the need for positive action and attitudes makes it imperative that parents be informed of the unique needs of their child, particularly as related to gifted behaviours, and the role they can play in the reversal process.

2. Teachers of gifted underachievers should be encouraged to advocate for the underachiever. In fact, according to these students, teachers at all grade levels play a major role in reversing underachievement. It appears that teachers who are seen as the most willing to help and are perceived as the most effective in learning situations exhibit many of the same characteristics as the subjects. These characteristics include their love of learning, commitment to task, personal involvement with the subject matter and the students.

3. Be patient. It will take time to reverse the patterns of underachievement. Hopes for the development of an intervention that offers immediate and permanent reversal of the underachievement pattern may be unrealistic and may inhibit the search for effective measures. Because of the many factors which can influence the onset and the reversal of underachievement, expect uneven progress and periodic setbacks when helping your gifted underachiever.

Be encouraged, as this study and others provide evidence that some forms of academic underachievement can be reversed.

Chapter 8
The Success Formula

In this chapter we will:

• determine how to identify your child's learning style and the development of the Learning Style Profile (LSP)

• examine how psychoeducational assessments (PEA) are done

• gain insight on the identification/diagnosis (Diagnosis) of the problem

• reinforce the importance of the grade report analysis (GRA) and of correcting identified problems to prevent additional ones

• focus on developing a prescription for your child's success.

• explain the formula [LSP+PEA+GRA = Diagnosis (D) + Prescription(P) + Remediation (R)]

Improving Your Childs' Academic Underperformance

I n the previous chapters, we looked at how to eliminate Learning Gaps such as those arising as a result of the COVID-19 Pandemic; the common types of learning disabilities/challenges; what to do and how to help your child deal with learning disabilities; the use of school reports in identifying concerns and reinforced the need to get the foundation right in order to prevent problems at other levels of the education system.

Let's turn our attention on developing a prescription for your child's success. The formula of [LSP+PEA+GRA = Diagnosis (D) + Prescription(P) + Remediation (R)] will now be fully explained.

Please note carefully that the information being presented is best utilized by professionals such as psychologists who will have a deeper appreciation of the concepts being shared. If as a parent you would like to learn how to use and apply the assessment on your child, additional training is available. Each child is unique, so while the principle remains the same, a unique prescription has to be developed for each of them. This is where the experts come in. However, I will share with you a synopsis of the process.

Six Steps for Reversing Academic Underperformance

Step 1 - Identify the child's learning style
- Identify the child's learning style - This is a test that reveals the child's dominant learning style. There are

several tools available online to assess learning styles. The Learning Style Survey by Maureen McKay provides both the survey and invaluable information that will assist you in determining your child's learning style and how you can help.

• When you know the child's dominant style of learning, you will be able to share this with the teachers. The information may also be used to choose the most appropriate strategy to help him or her learn.

Step 2 - *Take the child to a professional to get a psycho-educational assessment/evaluation- This assessment will reveal the source of the problem.*

• This assessment/evaluation may be conducted by a psychologist/school counsellor, Child Psychologists, Educational Psychologists, Counselling Psychologists and Clinical Psychologists.

• The counsellor will interview you and the child in order to identify the source of the problem.

• That professional may also need to work with other professionals to develop a unique system to resolve the child's problem. A child's abilities, capabilities (that which he or she can do, if taught how to do it), experiences from birth up to the point of the assessment, dominant style of learning, and any physical or intellectual challenges are all combined to create a picture of the learner.

• A psycho-educational assessment is an analysis of all the factors that are affecting the learning, retention, and academic performance of the student. They include the: (1) learner (2) learning process (3) learning situation or environment (4) teacher (5) evaluation of the learning or academic performance

Step 3 - Analyze past school/grade reports

• Analyze past school/grade reports to reveal trends or patterns of weaknesses that need to be addressed. In identifying and strategizing to solve those problems, correcting those deficiencies will provide a stronger foundation on which to build.

• Get a tutor - If significant areas of weaknesses are found, you may need to acquire a tutor to work with your child. The individual attention that will be given to the child as he or she hones those skills, will equip the child to advance to higher cognitive functions or tasks.

Step 4 – Secure a Diagnosis/identification of the child's problem

• Have the child tested psychometrically - If additional challenges are identified while the tutor works with the child or if the child is not advancing as expected, the child may have a learning disability that needs to be identified through Psychometric testing at an approved assessment centre.

Step 5 – Get a prescription for the child's success

• To solve the problem of academic underperformance, the results of the learning style profile, psychoeducational assessments and psychometric tests conducted along with the challenges identified from the review of the grade reports will be combined to prescribe or recommend a unique course of action. This Personalized learning plan (PLP) will guide the child's progress in reversing academic underperformance. The learning plan should include "daily actionable" goals, action steps, competencies, and recommendations for the speed at which each should take place. It will guide him/her on his/her learning journey and ensure that he/she accomplishes what he/she needs academically, socially, and emotionally.

Step 6 – Work with the Guidance Counsellor or School Social Worker to manage the process

• In order for the situation to improve, the team will need to work together to fix the various situations that resulted in your child's academic underperformance. If a social worker is assigned to your child's school this professional will coordinate the work of individuals providing care and support to the child. Where no social worker exists, the school's guidance counsellor needs to act as the liaison among the professionals. Where the guidance counsellor is unable to perform this task, you, the child's parent will have to do it.

In summary, the six steps towards the reversal of academic underperformance are:

• Step 1 - Identify the child's learning style and the development of his/her learning style profile (LSP).

• Step 2 – Take the child to a professional to get a psycho-educational assessment/evaluation (PEA).

• Step 3 – Analyze the grade reports (GRA) correcting identified problems in order to prevent additional ones.

• Step 4 - Secure a Diagnosis/identification of the child's problem (Diagnosis) - if the child has a problem, the types of problems and how and where to get help

• Step 5 - Get a prescription for the child's success.

• Step 6 - Work with the Guidance Counsellor or School Social Worker to manage the process.

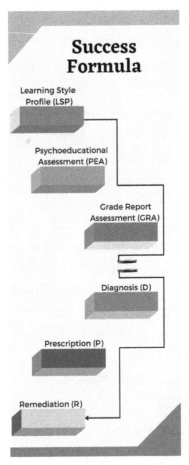

Diagram of the Success Formula: [LSP+PEA+GRA = D +
P + R]
Learning Style Profile [(LSP)+Psycho-educational Assessment
(PEA)+Grade Report Assessment (GRA) = Diagnosis (D) +
Prescription (P) and Remediation (R)]

The concepts of learning style profiles, psycho-educational assessment and grade report analysis were explained in a previous section. When all those elements are examined and thoroughly analyzed a diagnosis can be made. Compare this with what happens during a visit to your physician. The doctor asks you about the symptoms that prompted you to visit him/her, examines you physically and then based on his/her years of training and experience, makes a diagnosis, and gives you a prescription. You are then expected to fill the prescription, taking the medication as directed until the problem which prompted you to see the doctor is fully resolved.

Your child's mental health is managed in the same way. The psychologist with his/her training and years of experience will examine all those factors listed and make a diagnosis. The difference is that after the diagnosis and prescription is given the process of remediation/remedying the situation begins. This will take time and effort on the part of the child, the parent, and the school. If the school that your child attends does not have a social worker, request that they employ one.

> School social workers bring unique knowledge and skills to the school system and the student services team. They are trained mental health professionals who can assist with mental health concerns, behavioral concerns, positive behavioral support, academic, and classroom support, consultation with teachers, parents, and administrators as well as provide individual and group counseling/therapy. School social workers are instrumental in furthering the mission of the schools which is to provide a setting for teaching, learning, and for the attainment of competence

and confidence. School social workers enable the school to meet its academic mission, as home, school and community collaboration is the key to achieving student success (School Social Work Association of America, 2021).

As you seek to resolve the issue of academic underperformance, involve the professionals. Work with the team to identify the source of the problem and how to resolve it and the "village" will help you to raise your child effectively and well.

Chapter 9
After Exhausting School Resources, What Next?

In this chapter, we will explore external resources available to support your child. The following is an outline of the matters to be covered:

• Referrals: Understanding the role of various professionals in resolving problems identified

• Supporting your child in improving his/her academic performance

• Medical/psychological/socioeconomic challenges

I will introduce you to the tools for resolving the various problems identified. The concept of a team-based approach will be reinforced. You will be guided where to get help after exhausting school resources. The role of various professionals in resolving specific problems identified and the principle of collaborating with these professionals will be outlined. You will learn how to support your children's educational pursuits beyond the school environment.

Other challenges such as medical, psychological, and socioeconomic problems that affect learning, retention and general academic performance will be explored. Finally, the principle of acceptance will be outlined as there will be challenges which parents will face that they will not be able to have resolved. The chapter will conclude with a brief synopsis of the academic journeys of the children/families mentioned in this book.

Marie's Story

Marie has a child who is underperforming academically. She was called to a meeting at her daughter's school and advised to seek external intervention, as strategies employed by the school did not yield the intended results. She consulted with an Educational Psychologist who agreed to perform a psycho-educational assessment of her daughter. That arrangement fell through. She then attempted to see a Counselling Psychologist but was advised to see a Psychometrist in order to have the child tested for specific academic challenges. She has delayed getting that appointment as the cost was beyond her reach and her daughter's father, who did not believe the test was necessary, was not willing to pay to have it done.

You will agree that Marie is in a dilemma. What should she do?

Specialists Who Test for Learning Disabilities

- Psychologists: Clinical, School, Educational, Developmental, Counselling

- Child psychiatrists

- Neuropsychologist

- Psychometrician (person who tests for specific academic challenges)

- Speech and language therapist

- The Ministry of Education Special Education Unit

Would you go to your general practitioner to remove your teeth? What about the dermatologist doing heart surgery? No. Why then would you go to a pastor rather than a psychologist to solve your academic underperformance problems? Within the educational system, there are various specialists who are trained to deal with learning disabilities and challenges. Some educators specialize in helping special needs children and others to resolve psychological challenges that result in academic underperformance.

The following profiles of the professionals who are best equipped to manage various learning challenges were taken from the website of the American Psychological Association.

Counselling Psychologist

A Counselling Psychologist focuses on how people function both personally and in their relationships at all ages. A Counselling Psychologist addresses the emotional, social, work, school and physical health concerns people may have at different stages in their lives, focusing on typical life stresses and more severe issues with which people may struggle as individuals and as a part of families, groups, and organizations. Counselling psychologists help people with physical, emotional, and mental health issues improve their sense of well-being, alleviate feelings of distress, and resolve crises. They also provide assessment, diagnosis, and treatment of more severe psychological symptoms (APA, 2008).

Clinical Neuropsychologist

A Clinical Neuropsychologist works within a speciality field within clinical psychology. He/she is dedicated to understanding the relationships between the brain and behaviours, particularly as these relationships can be applied to the diagnosis of brain disorder, assessment of cognitive and behavioural functioning and the design of effective treatment. Neuropsychological evaluations are requested specifically to help understand how the different areas and systems of the brain are working. Testing is usually recommended when there are symptoms or complaints involving memory or thinking. This may be signalled by a change in concentration, organization, reasoning, memory, language, perception, coordination, or personality. The change may be due to any of a number of medical, neurological, psychological, or genetic causes.

Skills and Procedures Utilized

The neuropsychological evaluation consists of gathering relevant historical information, a neuropsychological examination, analysis and integration of data and findings, and feedback to the referral source. History is obtained through reviewing medical and other records, and through interviews with the patient. With the patient's permission, family members or other knowledgeable persons may be interviewed and asked to share their perceptions and perspective on important aspects of the history and symptoms. The examination typically consists of the administration of standardized tests using oral questions, paper and pencil, computers, the manipulation of materials such as blocks and puzzles, and other procedures. Depending on the scope and intent of the evaluation, testing may focus on a wide range of cognitive functions including attention, memory, language, academic skills, reasoning, and problem-solving, visuospatial ability and sensory-motor skills. The neuropsychologist may also administer tests and questionnaires concerning psychological aspects of mood, emotional style, behaviour, and personality (APA, 2008).

School Psychologist

A School Psychologist works with children, youth, families, and the schooling process. School psychologists are prepared to intervene at the individual and system levels and develop, implement and evaluate programs to promote positive learning environments for children and youth from diverse backgrounds and ensure equal access to effective educational and psychological services that promote healthy development.

Specialized Knowledge

Core knowledge is rooted in psychology and education and includes knowledge of psychoeducational assessment and diagnosis, intervention, prevention, health promotion, and program development focusing on children and youth development within the context of schools, families, and other systems. Knowledge of cultural contexts to address culturally or linguistically diverse individuals, and in learning and effective instruction, and family and parenting processes are critical. School psychologists:

A School Psychologist conceptualizes children's development and translates scientific findings to alleviate cognitive, behavioural, social, and emotional problems; have knowledge of federal law and regulations, case law, and state statutes and regulations for schools and psychological services;

appreciate historical influences of educational, community, state, federal, and organizational dynamics on academic, social, and emotional functioning (APA, 2008).

Clinical Psychologist

A Clinical Psychologist is a psychological specialist that provides continuing and comprehensive mental and behavioural health care for individuals and families; consultation to agencies and communities; training, education, and supervision; and research-based practice inclusive of severe psychopathology. He/she integrates knowledge and skill from a broad array of disciplines within and outside of psychology proper. The scope of work of the clinical psychologist encompasses all ages, multiple diversities, and varied systems (APA, 2008).

Child Psychiatrist

A Child Psychiatrist is a medical doctor concerned with the study and treatment of mental, emotional, and behavioural disorders of childhood. Although many of the general principles relating to the therapy of adult psychological disorders apply to child psychiatry, a major distinction is that the child psychiatrist must obtain much of the critical information about the child's behaviour from the adults who have been in frequent or close contact with the child—parents, paediatricians, psychologists, teachers, or social workers (Britannica, 2021).

Psychometrician

In our world obsessed with constant competition, placement, and proper development, testing has become a very common procedure. We have tests designed to determine how intelligent we are, as well as tests that group students together in classes that are within their mental capacity. We also have tests that tell us which jobs would be best for us, and we even have tests that claim to reveal our personalities. Chances are you've encountered at least one of these types of tests at some point in your life, but have you ever wondered where these tests come from and who designs them?

Psychometrics is the science of measuring people's mental capacities and thought processes in a systemized manner. In other words, it's a way to create tests to determine how smart we are or what our personalities are like.

Psychometricians are the scientists behind those interesting - and sometimes nerve-wracking - aptitude and personality tests. The tests that these professionals create help to better understand how the mind works. They are able to measure how a mind functions and how it compares to other groups of people.

Throughout the years, the original intelligence test has been changed slightly and adapted throughout the years. Today, this test is still used to measure a person's IQ, or how smart he is compared to his peers. Other tests have also been created, which can measure everything from a person's personality traits to what type of career he would excel at (Morrison, 2021).

Speech-Language Therapists

Speech-language therapists assess and treat people who have problems with verbal communication or swallowing. This may include difficulties with speech, language, listening, reading, or writing. They help children with a variety of conditions including mild, moderate, or severe learning difficulties, language delay, specific difficulties in producing sounds, hearing impairment, tongue-tied – ankyloglossia, stammering, voice disorders, selective mutism, and developmental language disorder (Reo a-Waha, 2020).

Guidance Counsellor

The Guidance Counsellor ensures that the school facilities which are in place are effectively utilized for the total development of the individual student, to enable him or her to lead a more fulfilling life. He/she develops services and programmes for the personal/social, educational, and career development of all students. In addition, he/she is responsible for several programmes including the HIV/AIDS Programme in Schools, the Programme for Alternative Student Support, the Safe Schools Programme and the Health and Family Life Education in Schools (Indeed.com, 2021).

Special Education Teacher

A Special Education Teacher is someone who works with children and youths who have a variety of disabilities. Children with special needs require unique instruction by specially trained professionals to help them achieve their highest potential and strive to progress beyond their limitations. Special education teachers are patient, understanding educators dedicated to giving each individual student the tools and guidance needed to help them maximize success.

A small number of special education teachers work with students with severe cognitive, emotional, or physical disabilities. Their job is primarily teaching them life skills and basic literacy. However, the majority of special education teachers work with children with mild to moderate disabilities, modifying the general education curriculum to meet the child's individual needs and providing required instruction. Most special education teachers instruct students at the preschool, elementary, middle, and secondary school levels, although some work with infants and toddlers.

Special Education Teachers work with students who have a wide range of special needs and disabilities. These specially-trained educators create and apply appropriate curricula and assign activities that are specific to each student's abilities and needs. Special education teachers also involve themselves in each student's academic, social, and behavioural development.

Special Needs Educators assist in developing Individualized Education Programs (IEPs) for each individual student. The Individualized Education Program is designed to develop individual goals for the student and is modified to the student's abilities and needs. Special Education Teachers go over the IEP with the child's parents, general education teachers, and school administrators. They work very closely with parents to keep them updated on progress and make recommendations to promote learning in the home.

A large part of a special education teacher's job involves communicating and coordinating with others involved in the child's well-being, including parents, social workers, school psychologists, occupational and physical therapists, school administrators, and other teachers (Careerexplorer.com, 2021).

School Social Worker

School Social Workers are trained mental health professionals with a degree in social work. They provide services related to a student's social and emotional life as well as adjustment to school and/or society. School Social Workers are the link between the home, school, and community in providing direct as well as indirect services to students, families, and school personnel in promoting and supporting students' academic and social success.

School Social Work Services

Related Services

• Participating in special education assessment meetings as well as individual educational planning meetings.

• Working with those problems in a child's living situation affect the child's adjustment in school. (home, school, and community).

• Preparing a social or developmental history on a child with a disability.

• Counselling (group, individual and/or family).

• Mobilizing family, school, and community resources to enable the child to learn as effectively as possible in his or her educational programme.

• Assisting in developing positive behavioural intervention strategies.

Services to Parents/Families

• Working with parents to facilitate their support in their children's school adjustment.

• Alleviating family stress to enable the child to function more effectively in school and community.

• Assisting parents to access programs available to students with special needs.

- Assisting parents in accessing and utilizing school and community resources (School Social Work Association of America, (n. d.).

Chapter 10
Success Stories

Here are brief updates on the academic journeys of the children mentioned in the book.

1. Analisa's grades have improved significantly as the pandemic enabled her to attend classes online with the support of her family. She is now preparing for the final exams

in the government established Primary Exit Profile (PEP) exams.

2. John and Michael have settled well in their respective high schools. Their grades have fallen since the pandemic, but their mom has plans to implement the strategies that she previously learnt to reverse the COVID-19 induced learning gaps.

3. Adrian's parents succeeded in placing him in a technical/vocational high school in proximity to their home and his father's workplace. He has settled well in school and is progressing well. His family is satisfied that he will be able to access the type of facilities that will cater to his learning style and natural abilities.

4. Marie's daughter finally got the recommended psychometric test. Her mother is waiting the results to customize the type of support that she will provide her at home. She is now preparing for the PEP exams and Mary anticipates that she will do well.

5. Rose successfully completed all her external CSEC SBAs and examinations and is extremely proud of her achievement. She has also received full acceptance to the university of her choice to study a degree in Hotel and Tourism Management.

As our journey comes to an end, let's explore the principle of acceptance and the challenges which some parents will face that they will not be resolved. I am sure you may also have asked if all academic underperformance and or challenges can be corrected? You may have also asked if all academic underperformances can be reversed or eliminated? The answer is, *no*. Many of us have heard the adage "every child can learn, every child must learn" or that "every child can learn, not just on the same day or in the same way." But are these statements true? Several years ago, Grant Wiggins (1998) reminded teachers that they cannot teach everything; and that it was also obvious that they could not use every teaching method or every form of assessment.

Our children are gifted differently. The theory of multiple intelligences focuses on the uniqueness of individuals and the fact that each child will perform differently in different areas of study. Gardner (1983) describes nine intelligences: verbal-linguistic, logical-mathematical, visual-spatial, musical, bodily-kinaesthetic, interpersonal, intrapersonal, naturalistic, and existential *(see Appendix B - The 9 Intelligences of Multiple Intelligence Theory)*. The distinctions among these intelligences are supported by studies in child development, cognitive skills under conditions of brain damage, psychometrics, changes in cognition across history and within different cultures, and psychological transfer and generalization.

As we examine the fact that our children are differently gifted, we need to bear that in mind as we assess their true potential. It is not always about academics. This means that as we look at academic underperformance, we need to look at the total child and how we can get them to use the gifts and talents with which they have been endowed as individuals.

Integrating the theory on learning styles with that of Howard Gardner's multiple intelligences can help children learn in many ways—not just in the areas of their strengths (Silver, Strong & Perini, 1997). These two theories attempt to interpret human differences and to design educational models around these differences. Both combine insights from biology, anthropology, psychology, medical case studies, and an examination of art and culture.

The theory of learning styles emphasizes the different ways people think and feel as they solve problems, create products, and interact. The theory of multiple intelligences is an effort to understand how cultures and disciplines shape human potential. Learning styles are concerned with differences in the *process* of learning, whereas multiple intelligences centre on the *content* and *products* of learning.

Howard Gardner (1993) opined that the integration of learning styles and multiple intelligence theory may provide some practical suggestions for teachers and parents to successfully integrate and apply learning styles and multiple intelligence theory in the classroom and at home.

Here are some ways to use the knowledge you have gained to improve your child's academic performance and achievement.

1. Use the knowledge of both theories as a compass. Keep a running record of the styles and intelligences your child uses regularly and of those he/she avoids. When a particular form of assessment doesn't work, offer him/her another choice.

2. Focus on one intelligence at a time. Offer your child a choice in one of the learning styles or urge them to do two assessments: one from a style they like and one from a style they would normally avoid.

3. Build on student interest. When your child conducts research, either individually or in groups, show him/her the options and allow them to choose the product or approach that appeals to them. She/he should choose the best product for communicating his/her understanding of the topic or text. In doing so, he/she will discover not only the meaning of quality, but also something about the nature of their own interests, concerns, styles, and intelligences.

If your child has a learning disability, do not lose hope. Many famous individuals have overcome those challenges and excelled in their various fields. Share the stories of the individuals below with your child and encourage him/her to maximize his/her potential in his/her area of giftedness.

- Thomas Edison - Inventor, had dyslexia and ADHD

- Albert Einstein – Mathematician, had dyslexia

- Whoopie Goldberg – Author/ Comedian, had dyslexia

- Earvin "Magic" Johnson – Basketball Player, had dyslexia

- Isaac Newton – Mathematician/Philosopher, had autism

- Mark Twain – Author, had a learning disability

- George Washington – 1st President of the United States of America, had dyslexia

- Elon Musk (Asperger) Entrepreneur and currently the world's richest man has Asperger

- Dr. Floyd Morris – 1st Blind Jamaican Senator

In conclusion, both multiple intelligences and learning styles can work together to form a powerful and integrated model of human intelligence and learning—a model that respects and celebrates diversity and provides us with the tools to improve academic performance or accept the challenges that cannot be changed.

Appendices

Appendix A: Learning Styles Quiz: What Is Your Child's Learning Style?

How Do I Learn?

Place a check (✔) in all the blanks that describe you. The list with the greatest number of checks is how you like to learn best.

Visual Learning Style

1. I remember best by writing things down or drawing pictures.

2. I ask for directions to be repeated.

3. I like to read about something rather than hear about it.

4. I am a good speller.

5. I like to learn with posters, videos, and pictures.

6. I am good at reading maps and graphs.

7. When someone is talking, I create pictures in my mind about what they are saying.

8. After school, I like to read books.

9. I like it when my teacher uses lots of pictures when teaching.

10. I can remember something if I picture it in my head.

How many checks (✔) did you have?

Remember to place a check (✔) in all the blanks that describe you.

Auditory Learning Style

1. I remember best if I hear something.

2. It is easier for me to listen to a story on tape than to read it.

3. I understand better when I read out loud.

4. I follow spoken directions well.

5. I like to sing or hum to myself.

6. I like to talk to my friends or family.

7. Music helps me learn things better.

8. I can easily remember what people say.

9. It helps when the teacher explains posters or pictures to me.

10. I can remember more about something new if I can talk about it.

How many checks (✔) did you have?

Remember to place a check (✔) in all the blanks that describe you.

Tactile/Kinesthetic Learning Style

1. I remember best if I can make something that tells about what I am learning.

2. I would rather play sports than read.

3. I like playing card or board games to learn new things.

4. I like to write letters or write in a journal.

5. I like it when teachers let me practice something with an activity.

6. I like putting together puzzles.

7. If I have to solve a problem, it helps me to move while I think.

8. It is hard for me to sit for a long time.

9. I enjoy dancing or moving to music.

10. I like to act things out to show what I have learned.

How many checks (✔) did you have?

Tell Me...

Which list had the most (✔) checks?

Which list had the fewest (✔) checks?

Did you have any lists that had the same number of (✔) checks?

If so, which ones?

Do you think the list that had the most checks (✔) tells how you like to learn best?

Appendix B: The 9 Intelligences of Multiple Intelligence Theory

	INTELLIGENCE	SKILLS AND CAREER PREFERENCES
1.	Verbal-Linguistic Intelligence Well-developed verbal skills and sensitivity to the sounds, meanings, and rhythms of words	Skills - Listening, speaking, writing, teaching. Careers - Poet, journalist, writer, teacher, lawyer, politician, translator
2.	Mathematical-Logical Intelligence Ability to think conceptually and abstractly, and capacity to discern logical or numerical patterns	Skills - Problem solving (logical & math), performing experiments Careers - Scientists, engineers, accountants, mathematicians
3.	Musical Intelligence Ability to produce and appreciate rhythm, pitch, and timber	Skills - Singing, playing instruments, composing music Careers - Musician, disc jockey, singer, composer
4.	Visual-Spatial Intelligence Capacity to think in images and pictures, to visualize accurately and abstractly	Skills - puzzle building, painting, constructing, fixing, designing objects Careers - Sculptor, artist, inventor, architect, mechanic, engineer
5.	Bodily-Kinesthetic Intelligence Ability to control one's body movements and to handle objects skillfully	Skills - Dancing, sports, hands on experiments, acting Careers - Athlete, PE teacher, dancer, actor, firefighter
6.	Interpersonal Intelligence Capacity to detect and respond appropriately to the moods, motivations, and desires of others	Skills - Seeing from other perspectives, empathy, counseling, co-operating Careers - Counselor, salesperson, politician, businessperson, minister
7.	Intrapersonal Intelligence Capacity to be self-aware and in tune with inner feelings, values, beliefs and thinking processes	Skills - Recognize one's S/W, reflective, aware of inner feelings Careers - Researchers, theorists, philosophers
8.	Naturalist Intelligence Ability to recognize and categorize plants, animals, and other objects in nature	Skills - Recognize one's connection to nature, apply science theory to life Careers – Scientist, naturalist, landscape architect
9.	Existential Intelligence Sensitivity and capacity to tackle deep questions about human existence, such as the meaning of life, why do we die, and how did we get here	Skills – Reflective and deep thinking, design abstract theories Careers – Scientist, philosopher, theologian

Appendix C: Checklist of Academic Underperformance

- The child does not complete assignments/homework and has no interest in doing so or doing it well.

- He/she refuses to do schoolwork.

- The child tells you that he/she could have done better on a test/assignment/project.

- The child has difficulty understanding, learning, remembering, or completing work assigned.

- His/her grades are lower than you expected, even if the grades are above the pass mark.

- His/her grades are low – below the pass mark or standard set by the teacher/school.

- He/she is performing below/way below that of his/her peers.

- His/her teachers state on the report that he/she has the potential to do better.

- His/her teacher tell you that the child can do better during parent-teacher consultation session.

- The school calls you in to discuss your child's academic underperformance.

Appendix D: Learning and Retention Techniques

Excerpts from the article "5 Research-Backed Studying Techniques" By Edward Kang

The techniques below will assist your child in learning what is being taught and retaining that knowledge for future use.

•*Pre-test:* When students practice answering questions, even incorrectly, before learning the content, their future learning is enhanced. Research_has_shown that pre-testing improves post-test results more than spending the same amount of time studying.

•*Spacing out study sessions:* Focus on a topic for a short period on different days—has been shown to improve retention and recall more. Creating flash cards that can be used for spaced practice and self-quizzing is effective. Students should create different piles when reviewing the flash cards. The cards they're able to answer immediately should be placed in a pile to review three days later; those answered with some difficulty should be reviewed two days later; and those that they answered incorrectly should be reviewed the next day.

•*Self-quizzing:* Testing has a negative connotation in this era of standardized testing, but it is a form of active_retrieval practice. Encourage students to make test questions for themselves as they learn a new concept, thinking about the types of questions you might ask on a quiz or test. They should incorporate these quizzes into their study sessions, answering every question, even those they believe they know well.

•*Interleaving practice*: An effective method of studying is to work on a set of problems that are related but not all of the same kind—for example, a set of math_word_problems that call for addition, subtraction, multiplication, or division. The consecutive problems cannot be solved with the same strategy. This is more effective than doing one multiplication problem after another.

•*Paraphrasing and reflecting:* Many of us have read a few paragraphs in a textbook only to realize that we didn't retain a single concept or key point presented in those paragraphs. To combat this, utilize intentional learning strategies. These include relating what is being learned to prior knowledge, thinking about how they would explain the content to a 5-year-old, and reflecting on and asking questions about the content.

Appendix E: Directory of Services

Help for Children with Learning Disabilities in Jamaica

- *Early Stimulation Programme*

  92 Hanover Street
  Kingston
  Telephone: (876)922-5585

- *Mico Child Assessment and Research in Education*

  5 Manhattan Road
  Kingston 5
  Telephone: (876)929-7720/754-4757

- *The Jamaica Association for Children with Learning Disability*

  7 Leinster Road
  Kingston5
  Telephone: (876)929-4341/929-4348

- *McCam Child Care and Development*
  231 Old Hope Road
  Kingston 6
  Telephone: (876)977-0189/977-6496

- *School of Hope*
  7 Golding Avenue
  P.O Box 224
  Kingston 7
  Telephone: (876)927-2054

- *Sure Foundation Educational Centre*
  15a Shortwood Rd., Kingston 8
  876-924-4495 | surefoundation05@gmail.com.
  www.dr.clararicketts.com

Online Resources for Supporting Learners with Disabilities

- *Accelerated Reader 360*

  Motivate, monitor, and manage students' independence in reading. Helps student practice and develop a love of reading.

- *Articulation Station*

  Help teach student how to pronounce the sounds in the English language with 6 engaging activities.

- *Autism Core Skills*

  Infiniteach Autism Core Skills teaches early academic, social, and communication skills that are interactive and engaging for verbal or nonverbal learners.

- *Bookshare*

For students with dyslexia, blindness, cerebral palsy, and other reading barriers, Bookshare is a free online library that provides access to over 800,000 eBooks in easy-to read formats. Students can read books in audio, follow text with karaoke-style highlighting, read in braille or large font, and customize their reading experience to suit their individual learning style.

- *BrainPOP*

BrainPOP's animated movies, creative thinking tools, interactive quizzes, and playful assessments have made a difference for millions of students. It can be assigned by a teacher and used independently by a student. Students must have a desktop or laptop computer and internet access – low bandwidth (e.g., for email, web searching, word processing).

- *Choiceworks Calendar*

The Choiceworks Calendar is a powerful picture-based learning tool that helps children learn what is happening day-to-day throughout each month. By presenting the abstract concept of time in a structured, visual format, Choiceworks Calendar helps children organize their lives as well as understand sequence and time.

- *Classworks*

Classworks provides students with an Individualized Learning Path focused on the skills and standards they are ready to learn. Each student's learning path is automatically informed by his or her assessment data from one of our nationally recognized partners or our NCII-validated screener.

- *LetterSchool*

LetterSchool's simple, consistent method shares strong clues with kids. This is aimed to assist and include all children, regardless of their learning styles. This way, the app is also ideal for children who reverse letters or numbers and special needs children.

- *Read and Write*

Help struggling students create and engage with content across all grade levels and subjects, optimizing their own personal learning styles.

- *Scan and Read Pro*

Scan and Read Pro is a fully powered scanning application that creates an electronic file for scanned documents. It comes complete with voice capabilities for reading, auditory highlighting, multi-lingual support, and summarization features. The program assists in reading and comprehension by highlighting each word as it is read aloud. Its easy-to-use graphical interface lets you change the appearance of the page to fit your individual needs, using your strengths to overcome any reading weaknesses.

References

American Psychological Association. (2014). *A career in counselling psychology*. Retrieved October 22, 2021 from https://www.apa.org/education-career/guide/subfields/counseling.

American Psychological Association. (2008). *Clinical Neuropsychology*. Retrieved October 22, 2021 from https://www.apa.org/ed/graduate/specialize/neuropsychology.

American Psychological Association (2020, August). *School Psychology*. Retrieved October 22, 2021 from https://www.apa.org/ed/graduate/specialize/school.

American Psychological Association (2008). *Clinical Psychology*. Retrieved October 22, 2021 from https://www.apa.org/ed/graduate/specialize/clinical.

Britannica, T. (2015, January 19). *Child psychiatry*. Encyclopedia Britannica. Retrieved October 22, 2021 from https://www.britannica.com/science/child-psychiatry

Butler, K. (1984). *Learning and Teaching Style in Theory and Practice.* Columbia, Conn.: The Learner's Dimension.

Careerexplorer.com. (2021). *What does a special education teacher do?* Retrieved October 22, 2021 from https://www.careerexplorer.com/careers/special-education-teacher/

Cogen, V. (1990). *Boosting the underachiever: How busy parents can unlock their child's potential.* New York: Berkley Book.

Emerick, L. J. (1992). Academic achievement among the gifted: students' perception of factors which reverse the pattern. In: *Gifted Child Quarterly.* Vol. 36, No. 3, pp. 140-146.

Gardner, H. (1983). *Frames of Mind: The Theory of Multiple Intelligences.* New York: Basic Books.

Gardner, H. (1993). *Multiple Intelligences: The Theory in Practice.* New York: Basic Books.

Hammill, D. D., Leigh, J. E., McNutt, G., & Larsen, S. C. (1988). A New Definition of Learning Disabilities. *Learning Disability Quarterly, 11*(3), 217–223. Retrieved from https://doi.org/10.2307/1510766

Indeed.com. (2021). *Guidance counselor job description: top duties and qualifications.* Retrieved October 22, 2021 from https://www.indeed.com/hire/job-description/guidance-counselor

Kang, R. (2019). 5 effective studying techniques that are backed by research. Retrieved October 22 from: https://www.edutopia.org/article/5-research-backed-studying-techniques

"Learning Style Survey for Young Learners" by Andrew D. Cohen and Rebecca L. Oxford and "Learning Style Survey" by Maureen McKay. Retrieved from https://www.teacherlists.com/blog/parent-corner/learning-styles-quiz-what-is-your-childs-learning-style/

Ludovici, J. (2015). *Improving Academic Underperformance® In College: A Multi-Factor Approach To Improving Grades And Helping Bright Students To Work Up To Their Potential. PA.*

Ministry of Education, Youth and Information. (2017). *Govt. looking to double tertiary enrollment by 2030.* Retrieved November 12, 2021 from https://moey.gov.jm/govt-looking-to-double-tertiary-enrollment-by-2030/

Moon, S.M. (2004). *Social/economic issues, underachievement, and counselling of gifted and talented students.* California: Corwin Press.

Morrison, C. (2021) *How to become a Psychometrician.* Retrieved October 22, 2021 from https://careersinpsychology.org/become-a-psychometrician/

Reading rockets: *Phonological and phonemic awareness.* Reading Rockets/Phonological and phonemic awareness (n.d.). Retrieved November 11, 2021 from https://www.readingrockets.org/teaching/reading-basics/phonemic

Reo a-Waha, K. (2020, December). Speech-language therapist. Retrieved October 22, 2021 from https://www.careers.govt.nz/jobs-database/health-and-community/health/speech-language-therapist/

Ricketts, C. (2019). *Yes They Can: Working with Children with Learning and Behavior Disorders.* Kingston, Jamaica: Extra Mile Innovators.

School Social Work Association of America. (n.d.). *Role of school social worker.* Retrieved October 22, 2021 from https://www.sswaa.org/school-social-work

Silver, H.F., and J.R. Hanson. (1995). *Learning Styles and Strategies.* Woodbridge, N.J.: The Thoughtful Education Press.

Silver, H.F, Strong, R. and Perini, M.J. (1997). Integrating learning styles and multiple intelligences. Retrieved October 22, 2021 from https://www.ascd.org/el/articles/integrating-learning-styles-and-multiple-intelligences

The Top 5 Common Learning Disabilities & Their Symptoms. Retrieved October 22, 2021 from https://www.ldrfa.org/the-top-5-most-common-learning-disabilities-their-symptoms.Types of Learning Disabilities.

Wiggins, G. and Mc Tighe, J. (2005). *Understanding by design.* VA, USA: ASCD.

About the Author

Dr. Viviene Kerr is the President of the Caribbean Graduate School of Theology (CGST) of which she is a graduate.

She has extensive experience in educational leadership, having earned a Doctor of Education degree from Nova Southeastern University. She presently lectures in the Department of Behavioural and Social Sciences at CGST.

Dr. Kerr is an experienced Educator, Counselling Psychologist, Librarian, Administrator, Advocate and Life Coach within the education and faith-based communities. She has a passion for helping individuals excel to their fullest potential.

She is presently (2021) the Vice Chairman of the National Parent Teachers' Association, Region 6 (St. Catherine, Jamaica); former president of the Home School Association and Parent Representative on the Board of Management of The Cedar Grove Academy.

Dr. Kerr is the mother of two children, who are both graduates of prominent high schools, and presently pursuing bachelor's degrees in aviation and hotel and tourism management respectively.

CPSIA information can be obtained
at www.ICGtesting.com
Printed in the USA
LVHW032238250122
709251LV00006B/101